GW00372030

Gallery Books
Editor Peter Fallon

THE MULTILINGUAL MERMAID

THE MULTILINGUAL MERMAID

Nuala Ní Dhomhnaill in Translation

Gallery Books

The Multilingual Mermaid:
Nuala Ní Dhomhnaill in Translation
is published in a limited
edition of 500 copies
on 30 November 2021.

The Gallery Press
Loughcrew
Oldcastle
County Meath
Ireland

www.gallerypress.com

ISBN 978 1 91133 824 6

A CIP catalogue record for this book
is available from the British Library.

The Multilingual Mermaid receives financial assistance
from the Arts Council.

Contents

Introduction

Nuala Ní Dhomhnaill is Ireland's best known and most widely translated poet writing in Irish. She is a key member of the talented group of poets who came together in University College Cork in the late 1960s and founded the literary journal *Innti* in 1970. This small group is generally credited with infusing Irish-language poetry with a counter-cultural, often urban, sensibility. Their conscious decision to write in Irish may be understood as a rebuke of the established Anglophone understanding of Irish identity and literature, a version that they wished to complicate and enrich from a multilingual perspective.

A defining feature of Nuala Ní Dhomhnaill's poetry is her recourse to mythology, folklore and oral tradition material, often reimagined through the lens of Jungian psychology. Her reimagining of older sources is often shot through with playful allusions and intertextual references from a variety of literatures and cultures. This is particularly apparent in the sequence of thirty-three poems based on the international folklore motif of the mermaid and titled 'Na Murúcha a Thriomaigh'. First published in 1998 in Ní Dhomhnaill's collection titled *Cead Aighnis*, this sequence was subsequently translated into English by Paul Muldoon under the title 'The Assimilated Merfolk'. Other possible translations of the original title include 'the merfolk who dried up', 'the merfolk who were washed ashore', 'the merfolk who were left high and dry' or 'the merfolk who fell silent'.

This extended sequence of poems, four of which are included in this anthology, examines the precarious existence of a population of mermaids (both male and female) who have been forced to leave their natural marine habitat and who are anxious to make a quick transition to life on land. The exact cause of their exodus is not revealed in the poems but the reader is left in no doubt as to the traumatic nature of the impetus and its long-term impact on the mermaids' physical and mental health. In the poem 'An Mhurúch san Ospidéal' ('The Mermaid in the Hospital') the mermaid wakes up, post-operation, to find that in place of her tail, she now has two legs. This physical transformation is only the beginning of the mermaid's journey as she learns to walk and to develop a new sense of self. The intergenerational consequences of displacement, as well as the painful attempt to suppress memories, is attested to in the poem 'Cuimhne an Uisce' ('A Recovered Memory of Water'). The mermaids' determination to assimilate entails jettisoning their native culture and language, a theme explored in the poem 'An Mhurúch agus Focail Áirithe' ('The Mermaid and Certain Words'). The lullaby sung by the mermaid-mother in the poem 'Leide Beag' ('A Tiny Clue') bears witness to the persistence of instinct: notwithstanding her desperate attempt to assimilate, native beliefs and value systems continue to shape the mermaid's understanding of reality, especially at those threshold or liminal points in life such as childbirth.

It is testimony to the international reach of Nuala Ní Dhomhnaill's work that she was awarded the Zbigniew Herbert International Literary Award in 2018, becoming the first female recipient of the award. The four mermaid poems, translated in this anthology into thirteen different languages, will resonate with international audiences as they address universal themes of forced displacement, culture shock, acculturation and traumatic memory in a manner that is deeply associative and compelling but not completely devoid of Ní Dhomhnaill's characteristic dark humour and lightness of touch.

Professor Ríóna Ní Fhrighil
Ollscoil na hÉireann, Gaillimh (NUI Galway)
July 2021

Translation Editor's Note

The Irish critic Denis Donoghue described his interpretation of literature as 'the intelligence that comes after'. Translation, too, is the intelligence that comes after the instigating imaginative event of the original. In the case of many of the translations here there's a double 'after' involved, in the sense that they are translations of translations, their primary relationship is with Paul Muldoon's own fruitful relationship with Nuala Ní Dhomhnaill's poems. Translation is an art born of elective affinity. Paul Muldoon's versions come out of a deep respect for the originals, but a respect that lends itself to a sparky, playful, inventive and never slavish engagement; his translations inhabit and perform these poems, and dress them in a lively and convincing English skin. Likewise the translators here, whether working from the originals or Muldoon's versions, are impelled by real enthusiasm for and joy in the strange, disturbing, tragicomic world of the stranded and psychically imprisoned merfolk, a subject which has imaginative resonance far beyond these shores. Some translators were put in mind of similar tales and motifs in their own languages, drawn to the work by common themes and resonances; others were drawn precisely because of the lack of anything like this work in their own cultures or by the paucity of female voices.

The challenge for the translators in crossing the linguistic divides is to capture the tone and registers of the originals, the sense of an underlying oral tradition and at the same time very modern sensibilities in the voices of the mermaids, as well as replicate in very different language contexts the rhythmic pulse in which those voices express themselves. Also to be dealt with are allusions to Irish tradition, culture and colonial history.

Translation is always a negotiated settlement, and nowhere is this truer than of poetry which functions on so many levels simultaneously. You might get the sense, but miss the music, or you might end up privileging the music at the expense of the poem's intent. Here, that tension can be doubled by linguistic remove: 'how does one pace a poem if one is not able to read the original text aloud?' one translator asks. Dependence on another poet's mediation is a risk, but it's a risk poets and translators often have to take. The reward in this case is locating the sense of shock at being in the wrong place, of being subject to a lifelong psychic displacement, in cultures which may have comparable experiences. Or, to paraphrase one of the translators here, the reward is finding that poetry grows gills to breathe at the crossroads where cultures intersect.

Peter Sirr
September 2021

Translator's Note

I translate Nuala Ní Dhomhnaill's poems for one very simple reason: I want to read them, and translation is the very closest form of reading of which we may avail ourselves. I studied Irish at school but am now very much out of the way of it, so the act of translation forces me to try to come to terms with one of the most interesting bodies of work in contemporary poetry. 'The Mermaid in the Hospital' is just one of a series of poems by Nuala Ní Dhomhnaill which I'm translating under the general title of *The Fifty Minute Mermaid*. As that title might suggest these poems feature merfolk who are at odds with themselves, psychologically as much as physically, in their dry land existences and are trying to make sense of their own translated lives.

One or two textual notes. The Irish phrase 'Oíche na Coda Móire', translated here as 'New Year's Eve', means 'the night of the large portion' and refers to the custom of feasting at New Year's in the hope of staving off fasting in the coming year. But there may be a bilingual pun on the word 'cod', in the fish sense, which might make a meal for the merfolk. The rather indelicate phrase 'arse-over-tip' is a lot less indelicate than the original, 'cocs-um-bo-head', a macaronic construction including a play on a slang term for the male member.

Paul Muldoon
2007

Cuimhne an Uisce

Uaireanta nuair a bhíonn a hiníon
sa seomra folctha
ag glanadh a fiacla le slaod tiubh
is le sód bácála,
tuigtear di go líonann an seomra suas
le huisce.

Tosnaíonn sé ag a cosa is a rúitíní
is bíonn sé ag slibearáil suas is suas arís
thar a másaí is a cromáin is a básta.
Ní fada
go mbíonn sé suas go dtí na hioscaidí uirthi.
Cromann sí síos ann go minic ag piocadh suas
rudaí mar thuáillí láimhe nó ceirteacha
atá ar maos ann.
Tá cuma na feamnaí orthu —
na scothóga fada ceilpe úd a dtugaidís
'gruaig mhaighdean mhara' nó 'eireaball mhadraí rua' orthu.
Ansan go hobann téann an t-uisce i ndísc
is ní fada
go mbíonn an seomra iomlán tirim arís.

Tá strus uafásach
ag roinnt leis na mothúcháin seo go léir.
Tar éis an tsaoil, níl rud ar bith aici
chun comparáid a dhéanamh leis.
Is níl na focail chearta ar eolas aici ar chor ar bith.
Ag a seisiún síciteiripeach seachtainiúil
bíonn a dóthain dua aici
ag iarraidh an scéal aisteach seo a mhíniú
is é a chur in iúl i gceart
don mheabhairdhochtúir.

Níl aon téarmaíocht aici,
ná téarmaí tagartha

A Recovered Memory of Water

Sometimes when the mermaid's daughter
is in the bathroom
cleaning her teeth with a thick brush
and baking soda
she has the sense the room is filling
with water.

It starts at her feet and ankles
and slides further and further up
over her thighs and hips and waist.
In no time
it's up to her oxters.
She bends down into it to pick up
handtowels and washcloths and all such things
as are sodden with it.
They all look like seaweed —
like those long strands of kelp that used to be called
'mermaid-hair' or 'foxtail'.
Just as suddenly the water recedes
and in no time
the room's completely dry again.

A terrible sense of stress
is part and parcel of these emotions.
At the end of the day she has nothing else
to compare it to.
She doesn't have the vocabulary for any of it.
At her weekly therapy session
she has more than enough to be going on with
just to describe this strange phenomenon
and to express it properly
to the psychiatrist.

She doesn't have the terminology
or any of the points of reference

ná focal ar bith a thabharfadh an tuairim is lú
do cad é 'uisce'.
'Lacht trédhearcach,' a deir sí, ag déanamh a cruinndíchill.
'Sea,' a deireann an teiripí, 'coinnibh ort!'
Bíonn sé á mholadh is á gríosadh chun gnímh teangan.
Deineann sí iarracht eile.
'Slaod tanaí,' a thugann sí air,
í ag tóraíocht go cúramach i measc na bhfocal.
'Brat gléineach, ábhar silteach, rud fliuch.'

or any word at all that would give the slightest suggestion
as to what water might be.
'A transparent liquid,' she says, doing as best she can.
'Right,' says the therapist, 'keep going.'
He coaxes and cajoles her towards word-making.
She has another run at it.
'A thin flow,' she calls it,
casting about gingerly in the midst of words.
'A shiny film. Dripping stuff. Something wet.'

An Mhurúch san Ospidéal

Dhúisigh sí
agus ní raibh a heireaball éisc ann
níos mó
ach istigh sa leaba léi
bhí an dá rud fada fuar seo.
Ba dhóigh leat gur gaid mhara iad
nó slaimicí feola.

'Mar mhagadh atá siad
ní foláir,
Oíche na Coda Móire.
Tá leath na foirne as a meabhair
le deoch
is an leath eile acu
róthugtha do jokeanna.
Mar sin féin is leor an méid seo,'
is do chaith sí an dá rud
amach as an seomra.

Ach seo í an chuid
ná tuigeann sí —
conas a thit sí féin ina ndiaidh
'cocs-um-bo-head'.
Cén bhaint a bhí
ag an dá rud léi
nó cén bhaint a bhí aici
leosan?

An bhanaltra a thug an nod di
is a chuir í i dtreo an eolais —
'Cos í seo atá ceangailte díot
agus ceann eile acu anseo thíos fút.
Cos, cos eile,
a haon, a dó.

The Mermaid in the Hospital

She awoke
to find her fishtail
clean gone
but in the bed with her
were two long, cold thingammies.
You'd have thought they were tangles of kelp
or collops of ham.

'They're no doubt
taking the piss,
it being New Year's Eve.
Half the staff legless
with drink
and the other half
playing pranks.
Still, this is taking it
a bit far.'
And with that she hurled
the two thingammies out of the room.

But here's the thing
she still doesn't get —
why she tumbled out after them
arse-over-tip . . .
How she was connected
to those two thingammies
and how they were connected
to her.

It was the sister who gave her the wink
and let her know what was what.
'You have one leg attached to you there
and another one underneath that.
One leg, two legs . . .
A-one and a-two . . .

Caithfidh tú foghlaim
conas siúl leo.'

Ins na míosa fada
a lean
n'fheadar ar thit a croí
de réir mar a thit
trácht na coise uirthi,
a háirsí?

Now you have to learn
what they can do.'

In the long months
that followed
I wonder if her heart fell
the way her arches fell,
her instep arches.

An Mhurúch agus Focail Áirithe

Ná luaigh an focal 'uisce' léi
nó aon ní a bhaineann le cúrsaí farraige —
'tonn', 'taoide', 'bóchna', 'muir' nó 'sáile'.
Ní lú léi an sioc samhraidh ná trácht a chlos
ar iascach, báid, saighní trá nó traimile, potaí gliomach.
Tá's aici go maith go bhfuil a leithéidí ann
is go mbíonn gíotáil éigin a bhaineas leo
ar siúl ag daoine eile.

Ceapann sí má dhúnann sí a cluasa is má chasann a ceann
go mbeidh sí saor orthu
is ná cloisfidh sí búir dhúr an eich uisce
ag fógairt gaoil shíoraí léi go doimhin san oíche,
ag cur gráinníní ar a craiceann is brat allais
amach trí lár a codladh uirthi.

Níl aon namhaid eile aici
ach an saol fó-thoinn a chleacht sí
sarar iontaigh sí ar a hathshaol ar an míntír
a chur i gcuimhne dhi. Séanann sí ó bhonn
go raibh oiread is cac snioga de bhaint aici leis
aon am. 'Ní raibh aon tsuim riamh agam
sna piseoga sin, nó in aon sórt seanaimsearachta.
Aer, eolas, solas gléineach na heolaíochta
is ea a shantaíos-sa.'

Ba chuma liom ach go bhfuaireas-sa amach
san éitheach í.

The Mermaid and Certain Words

Whatever you do don't ever mention the word 'water'
or anything else that smacks of the sea —
'wave', 'tide', 'ocean', 'the raging main', 'the briny'.
She'd as soon contemplate the arrival of frost in the middle
    of summer
than hear tell of fishing, boats, seine or trammel nets, lobster
    pots.
She knows that such things exist, of course,
and that other people
have truck with them.

She thinks that if she covers over her ears and turns away
    her head
she'll be free of them
and she'll never hear again the loud neighing of the kelpie
    or water horse
claiming its blood relation with her at the darkest hour of
    night,
causing her to break out in goose pimples and having sweat
    lashing off her
while she's fast asleep.

She hates nothing so much
as being reminded of the underwater life that she led
before she turned over a new leaf on dry land. She totally
    denies
that she had the slightest connection with it
at any time. 'I never had any interest
in those old superstitions, or any of the old traditions.
Fresh air, knowledge, the shining brightness of science
are all I ever hankered after.'

I wouldn't mind one way or the other but I myself have
    found her out
in the deception.

Istigh sa Roinn le Béaloideas Éireann,
tá lámhscríbhinn iomlán de Bhailiúchán na Scol
breactha óna láimh,
scríte in uisce, le clipe de sciathán rotha,
ar scothóg feamainne mar phár.

Tá trí cinn déag de scéalta fada
agus smutaíocha de chinn eile, i dteannta le
horthaí, seanphaidreacha, tomhaiseanna agus aroile
le tabhairt faoi ndeara ann.
Óna hathair is óna máthar chríonna is mó
a thóg sí síos iad.

Diúltaíonn sí glan dó — 'An máistir
a thug mar obair bhaile dhúinn é fadó
thiar sa bhunscoil. Chaitheamair é a dhéanamh.
Ní raibh aon dul as againn.'
Cháithfeadh sí fuil shróine
sara mbeadh sí riamh admhálach ina thionscnamh.

In the Department of Irish Folklore in University College,
     Dublin,
there is a whole manuscript in the Schools' Collection
that was set down by her,
written in water, with the fin of a ray for a pen,
on a long scroll of kelp.

In it can be found thirteen long tales
and odds and ends of other ones, together with
charms, old prayers, riddles and such.
From her father and her grandmother she mostly
took them down.

She refuses to accept its existence, and when she does,
     'It was the master
who gave it to us as homework, way back in the National
     School. We had to do it.
There was no getting out of it.'
She would prefer to suffer a heavy nosebleed
rather than admit she ever had a hand in its composition.

Leide Beag

Dá gcaithfeá faid do mharthana iomláin'
ag cúléisteacht leis an mhurúch
b'fhéidir go bhfaighfeá leide beag anseo is ansiúd
cárbh as di. Thángas-sa aniar aduaidh
uirthi lá fómhair is a naíonán
á bréagadh faoina seál aici.

'Ní tú éan gorm na mbainirseach,
ní tú gearrcach glas na gcaobach,
ní tú coileán an mhadra uisce,
ní tú lao na maoile caoile,'

an suantraí a bhí á chanadh aici
ach do stop sí suas láithreach bonn
chomh luath is a thuig sí
duine eile a bheith ar an bport.

Tuigeadh dom gur ghlac sí náire
i dtaobh é bheith cloiste agam in aon chor.
Tuigeadh dom chomh maith go raibh blas an-láidir
den bhfarraige air mar shuantraí ar an gcéad scór.

A Tiny Clue

You could spend your entire life
eavesdropping on the mermaid
before you'd pick up the tiniest little clue
about where she was really from. One autumn day
    I happened upon
her and her child
while she was comforting it under her shawl.

'You are not the blue-green pup of the seal.
You are not the grey chick of the greater black-backed gull.
You are not the kit of the otter. Nor are you
the calf of the slender hornless cow.'

This was the lullaby she was singing
but she stopped short
immediately she realized
someone else was in the neighbourhood.

I had the distinct sense she was embarrassed
I'd overheard her in the first place.
I also came away with the impression
the lullaby was, to put it mildly, redolent of the sea.

Translating into Arabic / عربي

Reflection by Asma Saad Alshammari and Awatif Alshammari

Nuala Ní Dhomhnaill's poems fascinated us as the motif of the mermaid forced to live on dry land seemed to us an effective metaphor for colonization. In Arabic culture, the figure of the mermaid is a symbol of female beauty while, in Arabic literary works, it is the desert that is central to authors' imaginations. The sea or aspects of maritime culture appear only in Romantic poems.

Translating the themes of psychological and physical trauma into another language and culture was challenging. There are many allusions to Irish tradition, culture, and colonial history in these poems that are very different from the Arabic context. We felt that we had to reimagine the content and context instead of translating literally. We did, however, pay close attention to the aesthetic and the many references to Irish folklore. We tried to preserve the Irish spirit of the poems while making them accessible to readers of Arabic. When we read Nuala Ní Dhomhnaill's poems we were reminded of the work of Arabic poet Mahmoud Darwish who writes about forced displacement, post-colonial struggles, and trauma. These themes appear in Ní Dhomhnaill's mermaid poems and will resonate with contemporary Arabic readers due to the experience of the colonization of Palestine land.

These translations are based on the English-language translations by Paul Muldoon.

An Mhurúch san Ospidéal
  The Mermaid in the Hospital

حوريَّةُ البحرِ في المستشفى

استيقظت

لتجدَ أنَّ ذيل الحوريَّةِ

قد اختفى

لكنَّها هناك في السرير معها

أحسَّت بقطعتين غريبتين باردتين طويلتين

ظنَّت بأنهما خيوطٌ متشابكةٌ من خيوط البحر

أو قطعاً من لحمٍ معجون

إنهم " بلا شَكٍّ "

مدعاة للسخرية

في ليلة تقديم القرابين (ليلة الاحتفال برأس السنة)

نصفٌ الموظفين بلا شركاء

مع شرابهم

ونصفهم الآخر

يضحكون ويمزحون

يأخذها ذلك بعيداً

ويدفعها لترمي

هذين الشيئين خارج الغرفة (وتمشي بهما)

لكنَّهما معها، شيئان غريبان

مازالت لا تفهم

لماذا هبطت بعدهم

وكيف هي تعلَّقت بهما

وكيف هما اتَّصلوا

بها

كانت أختها من أعطتها إشارةً (غمزةً)

وأخبرتها بالأمر الذي كان يحصل

" لديك ساقٌ متَّصلةٌ بك هنا

وواحدةٌ أخرى تحتها هناك

إن واحدة، وإن اثنتان

المهم أن تتعلمي الآن

كيف تستطيعين استخدامهما"

في الأشهر الطويلة

اللاحقة

أتساءلُ إذا سقطَ قلبها

بالطريقة نفسها التي سقطت بها أقواسها

أقواس مشط رجليها.

An Mhurúch agus Focail Áirithe
The Mermaid and Certain Words

حورِيَّة البحر وبعض كلماتٍ

مهما فعلتَ لا تذكر أبداً كلمة " ماء"

أو أيَّ شيءٍ آخر يتَّصل بالبحر

" الموج"، " المدُّ "، " المحيط"، " الهائجُ "، "حوريَّة".

سرعانَ ما فكَّرت بوقتِ وصول الصَّقيع في منتصف الصّيف

من سماع أخبار الصَّيد، القوارب، الشِّباك، وهياكل سرطان البحر.

إنها تعرفُ أن مثلَ هذا الأشياء موجودة، طبعاً!

وأنَّ هناك أناسٌ آخرون

يمتلكون الشَّحنات هناك.

تعتقد الحوريَّة أنَّها إذا غطَّت أذنيها وأبعدت رأسها

فإنَّها ستكون متحرِّرة منهم.

ولن تسمعَ صخب صوت كلب البحر أو حصان الماء

إذا صهلَ وهو يدَّعي أنه يرتبط معها بعلاقةِ دمِ في ليالٍ حالكةٍ

فتنهارُ مثل الوزَّةِ وتتعرَّقُ خجلاً وتنام بسرعةِ.

الآن لا تكرَهُ شيئاً

بقدر ما نكرهُ ما يذكِّرُها بالحياةِ تحت الماء التي أُرغمت عليها

قبل أن تصبحَ ورقةً جديدةً فوق اليابسة.

وهي التي تتبرَّأُ

من أي صلة سابقةٍ تربطها بها

في أيِّ وقتٍ سابقٍ. " لم يكن لديَّ أيُّ اهتمامٍ

بتلك الأساطير القديمةِ، أو التقاليدَ الباليةِ.

الهواءُ النَّقيُّ، المعرفةُ، العلم المشرقُ الساطغُ

تلك فقد كلُّ ما أتشَبَّثُ به..

أنا لا أمانعُ بطريقةٍ أو بأخرى، لكنني اكتشفتها بالخداع

وجدتها في الخارج

في قسم الفنون الشعبية الإيرلنديَّة

في كلية جامعة دبلن.

هناك مخطوطة كاملةٌ في قسم مجموعة المدارس

والتي قد كانت اودعتها هي هناك.

كُتبت تحت الماء مع زعانف من شعاع من القلم.

على لفيفةٍ طويلةٍ من عشب البحر.

ويمكن أن تعثرَ على ثلاثة عشر حكايةٍ طويلةٍ

واحتمالاتٍ ونهاياتٍ أخرى، جنباً إلى جنبٍ مع الساحرات، الصلوات القديمة،

وغيرها.

من والدها وجدَّتها إنها في الغالب أخذتهم إلى الأسفل.

إنها ترفضُ أن تتقبل وجودها، وعندما تفعل؛

" كان السيد الذي يعطينا إيَّاها كواجباتٍ منزليَّةٍ،

في طريق العودة من المدرسة الوطنية.

ونحن نقوم بها."

وقالت أنها تفضِّلُ أن تعاني من نزيفٍ شديدٍ بدلاً من الاعتراف بأنها تمتلك

يداً في تكوينها.

Cuimhne an Uisce
  A Recovered Memory of Water

استعادة ذاكرةُ الماء

في بعضِ الأحيان عندما تكون ابنة حورية البحر

في الحمام

تنظِّفُ أسنانها بصودا الخبز (كربونات الصوديوم)

تشعرُ بأنَّ الغرفة تمتلئ

بالماء.

يبدأ عند قدميها وكاحليها ثم ساقيها وركبتيها حتَّى يصل

فوق فخذيها وخصرها.

في غضون ثوان

يصل الماءُ الى ابطيها

فعندما تنحني لتلتقطَ

منشفة اليد أو منشفةَ الغسيل

وكل الأشياء المبللة

تشعر وكأنها كلها

تشبه الأعشابَ البحريَّة الطويلة وخيوطاً طويلةً تدعى

" شعرُ الحوريَّة" أو " فوكسفيل"

35

لكنَّ فجأةً يتراجع الماء

وفي غضون ثوان

تعودُ الغرفةُ جافَّةً تماماً.

شعورٌ بغيضٌ يعطي التوتر.

هذا الشعور الرهيب بالتَّعب ما هو إلَّا جزءٌ لا يتجزَّأ من مشاعرها.

في نهاية اليوم ليس لديها أيُّ شيءٍ آخر

لتقارنه بتلك المشاعر.

ليس لديها مفرداتٌ تصفُ مشاعرها.

في جلسة علاجها الأسبوعيَّة

لديها أكثر مما يكفي لتستمر

فقط في وصف هذه الظاهرة الغريبة

والتعبير عنها بشكلٍ صحيحٍ

لطبيبها النفسي.

ليس لديها مصطلحاتٍ

أو أي من النقاط المرجعيَّة

أو أيِّ كلمةٍ على الإطلاق تعطي أدنى فكرة

عن ماهية الماء بالنسبة لها.

" السائل الشفاف" كما تصفه، عندما تصفه بكلِّ ما في وسعها.

" صحيح" قال لها الطبيب، وتابع " أكملي".

يوجهها لتستطيع صنع الكلمات المناسبة.

لديها جولةٌ أخرى في هذا:

" تدفُّقُ رقيق" هكذا اسمته هذه المرَّة.

يلقي بالشَّغفِ بين الكلمات:

" فيلمٌ لامعٌ. أشياءُ تقطر. شيءٌ مبللٌ".

Leide Beag
A Tiny Clue

دليلٌ صغيرٌ

يمكنك أن تقضي حياتك كاملةً

تنصتُ لحورية البحر

قبل أن تلتقط أصغرَ دليلٍ

عن مكانها الحقيقي الذي جاءت منه. في يومٍ من أيام الخريف

حدثَ معي

هي وطفلها

بينما كانت ترتاح تحت وشاحها.

" أنت لست جرو الفقمةِ الأزرقِ والأخضر

ولست فرخَ النورس أسود الظهر

ولست عائلةً من القنافذِ. وكذلك لست

عجل البقرة التي لا تملك قرون"

هذه التهويدة التي تغنيها لها قبل النوم

لكنَّها توقَّفت فوراً

عندما أدركت

أن هناك شخصاً آخر في الجوار.

كان لديَّ إحساسٌ واضحٌ أنها محرجةٌ

من أنني استطعت سماعها في المقام الأوَّل.

وأعتقد أنني خرجت بانطباعٍ

أن تلك التهويدة كانت ـ بعبارة لطيفةٍ ـ "عبقُ البحر".

Translating into Chinese Mandarin / 汉语

Reflection by Li Yunru (李昀儒)

These poems are about history and memory. As a student of Irish studies I was particularly drawn to references to Irish mermaid folklore. I mostly applied literal translation techniques combined with some freer translation strategies, in order to maintain as many characteristics of Paul Muldoon's English versions as possible, while also making the poems understandable to Chinese readers.

The myth of mermaids has enchanted people around the world and the Chinese are no exception. These poems remind me of the folklore and tales about mermaids in the long history of China. The most beautiful one relates to the mermaids called 'Jiaoren'. In line with Irish imaginings, the ancient Chinese portrayed these sea creatures as beautiful women with human upper bodies and fish tails. It is believed that 'Jiaoren' are good at weaving and that the clothes they make are waterproof. In addition, their teardrops can turn into pearls as they fall. This folklore about mermaids is widely found and adapted in the Chinese literary tradition and artistic world. For example, Li Shangyin, an ancient poet in the Tang dynasty, invokes the myth of the Jiaorens' tears turning into pearls in his poem '沧海月明珠有泪', creating a mysterious atmosphere.

I was amazed to see how Irish and Chinese folk motifs resonate with each other. It will make a wonderful and meaningful experience to delve deep into the treasures of traditional Irish and Chinese cultures so as to endow the friendly relation between Ireland and China with multiple layers of connotations and understandings.

These translations are based on the English-language translations by Paul Muldoon.

An Mhurúch san Ospidéal
The Mermaid in the Hospital

人鱼在医院

她醒来
发现自己的鱼尾
杳无踪影
与她同床的
是两条瘦长、冰冷的腿。
你会以为那是缠绕的巨藻
或是一片一片的火腿。

'他们一定
在捉弄我
毕竟这是除夕夜。
一半人没有腿
喝着酒
另一半
在恶作剧
即使如此，这也
有些过分了。'
想到这里，她用力
想把两条腿扔出房间。

但事情是这样的
她始终不明白—

为什么她自己也跟着腿
摔了个四脚朝天……
她是怎么
和那两条腿相连
那两腿又是怎么
和她相连。

是她的姐姐向她使了个眼色
告诉她什么是什么。
'你有一条腿连着你那里
另一条在那之下。
一条腿，两条腿……
一条，两条……
现在你得学学
腿能做什么。'

漫长的岁月
接踵而至，
我想知道她的心是否失落
就像她的足弓陷下去，
脚背弓起来那样。

An Mhurúch agus Focail Áirithe
The Mermaid and Certain Words

人鱼和一些词

无论你做什么，千万别提'水'这个字
或任何暗示大海的内容—
'海浪'，'海潮'，'海洋'，'波涛汹涌'，'咸咸的海水'。
她宁愿在盛夏时节考虑霜冻的到来
也不愿听人讲捕鱼、划船、渔网、虾笼。
当然，她知道这些东西是存在的，
也有其他人
和它们打交道。

她以为如果她捂上耳朵，把头转向一旁
她就能得到解脱
就能不再听到水怪的嘶鸣着
在深夜之时，宣称和她有血缘关系，
使她起一身鸡皮疙瘩
睡梦中，吓出一身冷汗

她最讨厌
在这片干燥的土地上翻开新的一页后
有人提醒她之前的水下生活
她完全否认
和之前有丝毫联系
无论何时，'我从未对

那些老旧的迷信或古老的传统有任何兴趣
新鲜的空气、知识、科学的闪亮
才是我毕生所求。'

我不介意她说的这样或那样，但我发现
她骗人。
在都柏林大学
爱尔兰民俗系，
学校的收藏中有一份完整的手稿
是她写的，
在水里，用鱼鳍作笔，
写在一卷长长的海带上。

里面有十三个故事
和一些其他零碎的东西
符咒、古老的祈文、谜语等等。
来自她的父亲和祖母，
大多数她都记下来了。

她拒绝承认这手稿，被逼无奈时她会说，
'这是国际学校的老师
给我们的作业。
我们别无选择。'
她宁愿流鼻血
也不愿承认自己交过这份作品。

Cuimhne an Uisce
A Recovered Memory of Water

对水的记忆失而复得

有时人鱼的女儿
在浴室
用大牙刷和小苏打
清理牙齿
她有一种感觉
房间里充满了水。

先是在脚底和脚踝
慢慢地上升
到大腿、臀部和腰间。
不一会儿
就到了腋下
她弯下腰，浸入水中，
去捡手巾和毛巾之类的
都湿透了。
看起来像海草一
就像以前叫做海藻长丝一样，
　'美人鱼的头发"或"狐狸尾巴'。
水突然退去
很快
房间又完全干了。

一种可怕的紧张
占据心头。
到头来
也无法比拟。
没有言语能说清。
每周心理治疗时
有太多太多要说
只为描述这个奇怪现象
只为给医生说清。

她没有专业术语
没有参考文献
或任何提示
来帮她说清楚水是什么。
　'一种透明的液体'，她说，尽她所能。
　'对的'，医生说，'继续'。
他引导她继续造词。
她又试一次。
称之为'细流'，
小心翼翼地在字里行间转来转去。
　'闪烁的薄膜。滴滴答答的玩意儿。湿湿的东西。'

Leide Beag
  A Tiny Clue

小小的提示

你可以用你的一生
偷听这个人鱼的故事
之后你会得到一个小小的提示
关于她真正的家乡。一个秋日
我碰见她和她的孩子
她正在披肩之下安抚孩子。

　'你不是蓝绿相间的海豹幼崽。
不是大黑背鸥的灰色雏鸟。
不是水獭的宝宝，
也不是那头瘦长无角牛的孩子。'

这是她唱的摇篮曲
但她突然停顿
猛然意识到
有人在附近。
我明显感到她有些尴尬
我一开始就在偷听她讲话。
我离开的时候有这样的印象
那只催眠曲，婉转地说，使人想起大海。

Translating into Czech / Čeština

Reflection by Martin Světlík

Nuala Ní Dhomhnaill's poetry has always struck me as being poised between the mundane and the mythical, balancing the directness of a casual conversation with the intimations of an unspoken tale. That, at least, was my experience reading her poems about *murúcha* (merfolk), full of careful shifts of tone, subtle humour, and a deep sense of loss seeping through the façade of everyday experience. As a translator I realized I had to tread the delicate path between a colloquial expression and a crude one, to retain the ingenuity of the original without being too clever about it, and to convey the sense of fragility and trauma, yet resist the temptation of unnecessary pathos.

It has often been said that every translation involves a distortion of the original, if only ever so slight. The translator, however, may not always be entirely to blame for such shortcomings, especially when the text travels a long distance, not only in terms of language, but also in terms of culture and geography. For instance, despite what Shakespeare would have us believe, there is no sea coast in Bohemia, and I would argue that the image of the sea works differently in a landlocked country like Czechia, and in Ireland. In the former, it serves as shorthand for adventure, the exotic and perhaps the unattainable; in the latter its familiarity allows it to be, rather paradoxically, a constant reminder of the unknown, or forgotten.

Yet I believe that the careful balance between immediacy and profundity allows Nuala Ní Dhomhnaill's work, though steeped in the local tradition, to transcend cultural differences and be truly universal in its appeal and impact. In this respect I am happy to increase the number of voices through which her poems can speak to their readers.

These translations are based on the original Irish-language poems.

An Mhurúch san Ospidéal
The Mermaid in the Hospital

Mořská panna v nemocnici

Procitla
a rybí ocas byl
ten tam.
V posteli s ní ale ležely
dlouhé, chladné kusy čehosi.
Člověk by řekl snad chaluhy
nebo dvě flákoty.

„Jasně, to si ze mě dělaj
dobrej den —
— co naplat, silvestrovská noc.
Půlka personálu
na šrot
a druhá si dělá
šprťouchlata.
Ale stejně, tohle už je troche moc!"
A ty dva kusy čehosi
letěly z pokoje.

Jedna věc jí ale
Nejde do hlavy —
čím to, že za nimi letěla taky,
„vocasem napřed".
Jak s ní jenom souvisely
ty dva kusy čehosi
nebo jak ona souvisela
s nimi?

Sestra jí nakonec naznačila,
jak se věci mají —

„Jedna noha ti začíná tady
a druhou máš hned pod ní.
Jedna noha,
druhá noha,
za chvíli už
budeš běhat."

Přemýšlím, jak poté, během těch
dlouhých měsíců,
přenesla přes srdce
přenášet váhu z nohy
na nohu.

An Mhurúch agus Focail Áirithe
The Mermaid and Certain Words

Mořská panna a jistá slova

„Voda" — to slovo před ní neříkej,
nebo cokoliv jiného, co zavání mořem —
— „vlny", „odliv", „příliv", „moře", „sůl".
To raději připustí, že v létě bude chumelit, než poslouchat
o rybářích, lodích, vatkách či vězencích na humry.
Ano, takové věci jsou, to sama dobře ví,
a ostatní lidé s nimi mají
co do činění.

Myslí, že když si zakryje uši a odvrátí tvář,
bude mít od nich navždy pokoj,
že neuslyší mořského koně, jehož řehtání
jí za hluboké noci připomíná to odvěké pouto,
až jí ve spánku naskočí husí kůže
a polije studený pot.

Nezná nic horšího,
než když jí někdo připomene, jak kdysi
žila pod hladinou, před tím, než na pevnině
chytla druhý dech. Zásadně odmítá,
že by s tím vším měla cokoliv kdykoliv
společného. „Mně byly vždycky tyhle
starodávné zvyky a pověry úplně ukradené.
Vzduch, rozum, osvícená věda,
to bylo odjakživa moje krédo."

Já bych jí I věřila, kdybych ji sama nepřistihla,
jak lže.
Ve školních sbírkách Ústavu irského folkloru
je uložen dokument pořízený
její vlastní rukou,

psaný vodou a kostí z rejnočí ploutve
na kus řasy místo papíru.

Zapsáno je tam třináct dlouhých příběhů,
pár zlomků dalších vyprávění, společně
s kouzly, zaříkadly a tak dále.
Většinu zapsala
od svého otce a prababičky.

Naprosto bez obalu to všechno popírá — „To nám
kdysi dávno, ještě na škole, zadal učitel
jako domácí úkol. Museli jsme.
Z toho se člověk nevyvlíkl."
To by snad raději začala krvácet z nosu,
než přiznat, že by v tom všem kdy měla prsty.

Cuimhne an Uisce
A Recovered Memory of Water

Vzpomínka na vodu

Čas od času, když si její dcera
v koupelně
čistí zuby hustými vrstvami
prášku na pečivo,
má pocit, že se koupelna naplňuje
vodou.

U nohou a kotníků to začíná
a stoupá výš a ještě výš
přes stehna, boky a pas.
Zanedlouho
sahá až po ramena.
Většinou se sehne, aby sebrala
ze země ručníky, hadry a další věci,
celé mokré a nasáklé.
Vypadají jako mořské řasy —
ty dlouhé kusy chaluh, kterým se kdysi říkávalo
„vlasy mořské panny" nebo „slané lupení".
Najednou voda začne klesat
a zanedlouho
je celá koupelna opět suchá.

Tyhle pocity
jdou ruku v ruce se strašlivou úzkostí.
Konec konců není přece nic,
k čemu by to mohla přirovnat.
Chce všechno nějak popsat, ale nemá slov.
Týden co týden chodí na terapii
a láme si hlavu nad tím
jak jen tu divnou věc vyjádřit, vysvětlit,

aby to pochopil
i psycholog.

Chybí jí patřičný pojmový aparát,
nemá žádný výchozí bod,
nezná slovo, které by poskytlo byť mlhavou představu,
co je to „voda".
„Průzračná kapalina," snaží se ze všech sil.
„Dobře," říká terapeut, „jen tak dál!"
Chválí a povzbuzuje, vede ji ke slovním výlevům.
„Slabý proud" napadne ji,
zatímco opatrně našlapává mezi slovy.
„Zářivá vrstva. Něco, co kape. Mokrá věc."

Leide Beag
  A Tiny Clue

Sebemenší podezření

Celý život byste mohli
naslouchat mořské panně,
aniž byste pojali sebemenší podezření,
co je vlastně zač. Jednoho podzimního dne
jsem ji zaslechla, jak v šále
kolébá své dítě.

„Kdepak tuleňátko zelenavé,
kdepak šedé raččí holátko,
ty nejsi mládě mořské vydry,
komolé kravky telátko,“

zpívala mu do spánku.
Rázem ale zmlkla,
když si povšimnula,
že na břehu není sama.

Nejspíš se zastyděla,
že jsem ji vůbec slyšela zpívat.
Přišlo mi také, že ten nápěv
byl hned na první poslech cítit solí.

Translating into Dutch / Nederlands

Reflection by Benjamin Van Pottelbergh

Nuala Ní Dhomhnaill's merpeople poetry is imbued with a breathless sense of wonder and nautical nostalgia. I was immediately attracted to the poem 'Cuimhne an Uisce' ('A Recovered Memory of Water'), which recounts a young mermaid's search for the meaning of water and her struggle with sudden bathroom-flooding panic attacks. The unsettling, almost claustrophobic opening of the poem contrasts sharply with its final verse which takes the reader along to one of the mermaid's therapy sessions. The conversational style of this last verse feels refreshing and brings a light-hearted, almost soothing touch to the poem. Nuala Ní Dhomhnaill excels at juggling the semantics of a seemingly mundane concept like water and kindly invites the reader (and translator) to play along and ultimately co-construct the mermaid's memory and identity.

In my translation, I tried to remain loyal to the rhythm and sound patterns of Paul Muldoon's English translation. A good example of this is my translation of the phrase 'a terrible sense of stress' into 'een weerzinwekkende zenuwachtigheid' in the third verse. The st-string has been replaced with a wz-string to mimic the fickle murmur and discomfort of the original. I also included a number of water-related idioms in my translation, such as the verb 'wegebben' (to ebb away) in the second verse or the verb 'hengelen' (to angle) in the final verse. Finally, I introduced several explicit verbs in the second verse: 'woelen' (to churn), 'glibberen' (to glide) when the water touches the mermaid's feet and legs, and even 'likken' (to lick) when the water reaches her armpits. These three verbs all contribute to the intimate and claustrophobic feeling of complete submersion during the mermaid's panic attack.

This translation is based on the English-language translation by Paul Muldoon.

Cuimhne an Uisce
A Recovered Memory of Water

Een opgeduikelde herinnering aan water

Af en toe, wanneer de meermindochter zich
in de badkamer begeeft
haar tanden boent met een grove borstel
en baksoda
waant ze zich in een kamer gevuld
met water.

Het water woelt rond haar voeten en enkels
glibbert geleidelijk verder omhoog en omhoog
langs haar dijen en haar heupen en haar middel.
Vliegensvlug
likt het haar oksels.
Ze hurkt erin neer om
handdoeken en washandjes en van alles bijeen te rapen
doorweekt van het water.
Het lijkt net zeewier —
van die lange algenplukken die we
'meerminharen' en 'vossenstaarten' noemden.
Plotseling ebt het water weg
en voor ze het doorheeft
is de kamer opnieuw volledig droog.

Een weerzinwekkende zenuwachtigheid
is schering en inslag tussen haar emoties.
Hoe dan ook kan ze het nergens
mee vergelijken.
Ze heeft er simpelweg de woordenschat niet voor.
Tijdens haar wekelijkse therapiesessie
moet ze hemel en aarde bewegen
enkel om dit vreemde fenomeen te omschrijven

en het fatsoenlijk uit te drukken
aan de psychiater.

De terminologie ontglipt haar
en ieder referentiepunt
en ieder woord dat nog maar de subtielste hint geeft
over wat water volgens haar is.
'Een doorzichtige vloeistof', zegt ze, zet ze haar beste
   beentje voor.
'Goed zo', zegt de therapeut, 'ga zo door.'
Hij animeert haar, inspireert haar om woorden te vormen.
Ze probeert het nog een keertje.
'Een dunne stroom', noemt ze het,
terwijl ze behoedzaam hengelt in een zee van woorden.
'Een fonkelende film. Druppelend spul. Nattigheid.'

Translating into French / Français

Reflection by Audrey Robitaillié and Daniel McAuley

Unlike Charles Baudelaire, who in his poem 'L'Homme et la mer' insists that free people should cherish the sea, Nuala Ní Dhomhnaill's relationship with the ocean in her verse is an ambiguous one. Her mermaid poems question the linguistic and psychological border-crossings that displacement entails. Our challenge was to convey these issues as authentically as possible by recreating the wordplay and figures of speech used in the original Irish, producing a set of texts that stands alone in French reflecting, independently of the source, the pervasive imagery of water. In the French translations we draw heavily on the lexical field of the sea, already omnipresent, despite the mermaids' protestations, in the original poems. For instance, we choose to translate 'tar éis an tsaoil' (after all) as 'en bout de ligne', which is a Québécois phrase rather than one from France because of the fishing connotations of 'ligne'. To translate the puzzling 'slaod tiubh' in the poem 'Cuimhne an Uisce' ('The Recovered Memory of Water'), we choose the oxymoronic phrase 'flot épais,' more explicitly watery than 'slaod,' which is suggestive of a flowing substance. In 'An Mhurúch agus Focail Áirithe' ('The Mermaid and Certain Words'), the mermaid outwardly rejects her undersea life, but is found out by the narrator. We added water-related idioms to reflect this tension: 'vagues de sommeil,' 'laisser de glace,' 'n'avoir goutte à voir'.

These translations gave us an opportunity to revisit our French lexicon of the sea, returning to our coastal roots in Northern Ireland, Normandy and Brittany. The moiled cow of the lullaby in 'Leide Beag' is turned into Normandy cattle, the transposition still reflecting both the hornless features of the original Northern Irish animal and its possible exoticism for the Kerry poet. Our collaborative approach allowed us to play with various possible readings in both the source and target languages, taking opportunities to adapt and insert images in keeping with the original, and perhaps at times replacing areas where more direct translations lost the overall tone.

These collaborative translations are based on the original Irish-language poems.

An Mhurúch san Ospidéal
The Mermaid in the Hospital

La Sirène à l'hôpital

Elle se réveilla
et sa queue de poisson n'était
plus là
mais dans son lit
elle trouva ces deux trucs longs et froids.
On aurait dit des gigots
ou des nœuds de goémon.

« Ils s'en fichent,
je t'avoue,
c'est le Réveillon.
La moitié de l'équipe festoie,
bourrés,
et les autres loustics
sont en train de faire des farces.
Mais avec tout ça ils exagèrent, quand même. »
Et elle jeta les deux trucs
hors de la chambre.

Mais voilà ce qu'elle
ne comprit pas :
comment elle aussi,
la tête la première,
les suivit.
Quelle connexion avait-elle avec eux,
Quel était le lien entre eux et elle ?

Une infirmière lui fit signe,
Lui apprit :
« Voilà une jambe,
Et une autre aussi, attachées ici sous les hanches.

Une jambe, puis une autre,
une, deux.
Vous devez apprendre
à marcher avec elles. »

Durant les longs mois
qui suivirent ce moment,
l'envoûtement de son cœur
s'affaissait au fur et à mesure
que le faisaient
ses voûtes plantaires.

An Mhurúch agus Focail Áirithe
The Mermaid and Certain Words

La Sirène et certains mots

Ne mentionnez pas le mot « eau » devant elle
ou rien qui n'ait à voir avec la mer -
« vague », « lame », « océan », « flots », ou « marée ».
Entendre parler de la pêche, bateaux, filets, nasses,
casiers à homards la laisse de glace.
Elle sait bien que pareilles choses existent
et que d'autres les bricolent d'habitude.

Elle croit que si elle se bouche les oreilles et si elle détourne
    la tête,
elle en sera libre
et n'entendra pas le puissant hennissement du cheval de mer
qui lui rappelle leurs liens éternels au fond de la nuit,
par-delà les vagues de sommeil qui l'assaillent.

Elle n'a pas d'autre ennemi que le vif souvenir
de la vie sous-marine à laquelle elle était habituée
avant qu'elle ne se tourne vers cette nouvelle vie sur terre.
Elle renie fondamentalement avoir eu goutte
à voir avec cette autre vie.
« Je n'ai jamais été intéressée par ces superstitions, ou
    quelque autre vieillerie.
L'air, le savoir, la lumière resplendissante de la science
sont tout ce que j'ai toujours désiré. »

Cela me serait égal, mais j'ai moi-même mis au jour ses
    mensonges.
Dans les archives du Département de Folklore,
il y a des manuscrits entiers de la Collection des Écoles
de ses propres pattes de mouche,

couchées à l'encre océane, avec un stylet en aileron de raie,
sur une guirlande de goémon pour parchemin.

Il y a treize longs récits
et d'autres fragments par ci, par là, au milieu de
sorts, vieilles prières, énigmes et cætera
qui attirent l'attention.
Elle les tenait surtout
de son père et sa grand-mère.

Elle en fait table rase : « Le maître
nous les avait donnés comme devoirs autrefois
à l'école maternelle. Nous devions le faire.
On ne pouvait pas y échapper. »
Elle préférerait un nez ensanglanté
plutôt que d'admettre qu'elle est impliquée dans leur création.

Cuimhne an Uisce
A Recovered Memory of Water

La Mémoire de l'eau

Parfois quand sa fille est
dans la salle de bain
pour se laver les dents avec un flot épais
et du bicarbonate de soude,
elle a l'impression que la pièce se remplit
d'eau.

Ça commence à ses pieds et ses chevilles
puis le flot fluctuant monte, monte
au-dessus de ses cuisses, ses hanches et sa taille.
Il ne faut pas longtemps
pour que l'eau monte au creux de ses genoux.
Elle se penche souvent pour y ramasser
des choses comme des serviettes éponge
ou des guenilles trempées.
Elles ressemblent à des algues —
les longues fleurs des algues brunes qu'on traitait
de « cheveux de sirène » ou de « queues de renard ».
Ensuite, tout d'un coup, la source tarit
et en un instant
la pièce entière s'assèche à nouveau.

Chacune de ces émotions provoque
une angoisse terrible.
Incomparable, en bout de ligne.
Et elle n'a pas les mots justes de toute façon.
Pendant son rendez-vous hebdomadaire de psychothérapie
c'est assez difficile pour elle
d'essayer d'expliquer cette histoire étrange
et de la clarifier
pour le psychiatre.

Elle n'a pas le vocabulaire,
ni les termes de référence
ni les mots pour tenter de se former la moindre opinion
de ce qu'est « l'eau ».
« Du lait transparent », dit-elle, en faisant de son mieux.
« C'est ça, dit le thérapeute, continuez ! »
Il la complimente et la félicite de son effort linguistique.
Elle essaie encore.
« Les bas-fonds, » ajoute-t-elle,
concentrée pour la trouver dans cette marée de mots.
« Un voile scintillant, une matière ruisselante, quelque
    chose de mouillé. »

Leide Beag
A Tiny Clue

Un petit indice

Si tu passais toute ta vie
à écouter aux portes chez la sirène
il se pourrait que tu glanes ici ou là des petits indices
sur ses origines. Je l'ai prise au dépourvu
un jour d'automne en train de cajoler
son enfant sous son châle.

« Tu n'es ni le petit, bleu-vert, de la maman phoque,
ni l'oisillon gris de la goélande,
tu n'es ni le jeune de la loutre de mer,
ni le veau de la fine vache normande. »

Cette berceuse, elle la chantait
quand soudain elle s'est tue
dès qu'elle a senti
qu'il y avait quelqu'un.

J'ai compris qu'elle avait honte
que je l'aie entendue.
J'ai compris aussi que la chanson
sentait fort la mer de toute façon.

Translating into Galician / Galego and Spanish / Español

Reflection by Jorge Rodríguez Durán

I first came across Nuala Ní Dhomhnaill's poetry in my last year at university and she has become one of my favourite Irish poets since. I was quickly drawn to her writing because I was able to find a lot of common themes and yearnings between Ní Dhomhnaill's poetry and that of some Galician poets, such as Luz Pozo Garza, whose work Ní Dhomhnaill translated for the volume *To the Winds Our Sails: Irish Writers Translate Galician Poetry* (Salmon Poetry, 2010). Both poets use the mythological past in order to talk about contemporary society. Also, other poets such as Susana Sanches Arins, Emma Pedreira or María Lado rely strongly on the female experience and use references to water or the sea in imagining Galician identity.

For my translations I relied on the English versions by Paul Muldoon. However, coming from a linguistic minority in Spain, I also wanted to access as much of the original Irish text as possible with the help of Irish-speaking friends. The similarities between the Galician sensibility towards the importance of language and certain words in the poems and the deep connection with myths made Nuala Ní Dhomhnaill the obvious choice to contribute to the Aistriú project. Although some aspects may have been difficult to translate, as can happen in any translation, I feel that the soul of each poem has been preserved in my versions. Whenever I found it impossible to keep the same cultural references I tried to search for an equivalent in Galician or Spanish culture to help readers understand Ní Dhomhnaill's references as much as possible.

Even though Spanish and Galician are very similar Romance languages and I worked on both translations at the same time I tried to give each its own unique personality and rhythm. Although I wanted to keep as much as possible from the source texts in both translations, I also wanted to explicitly create a divergence between Spanish and Galician cultures and the way the main ideas in the texts would be received differently by the speakers of those languages. For 'Las sirenas encalladas' ('The Stranded Mermaids' in Spanish), for example, I decided to lean towards a vocabulary that would evoke merfolk from a mythological and perhaps fairy-tale-like perspective. 'As sereas enxoitas' ('The Dry Mermaids' in Galician) brings a more Atlantic feel to the text and deals in more depth with the relation to water and speech, especially in the poem 'An Mhurúch agus Focail Áirithe' ('The Mermaid and Certain Words').

These translations are based on the English-language translations by Paul Muldoon, with a few sections translated from the Irish source text in consultation with an Irish speaker.

An Mhurúch san Ospidéal
The Mermaid in the Hospital

A serea no hospital

Cando espertou
atopou no canto da súa cola
un corte limpo
e ao seu carón na cama
dous entes descoñecidos
a medio camiño entre un barullo de algas
e un xamón cocido.

'Están de broma.
Debe ser aninovo, a metade dos empregados
estarán xa bébedos,
e a outra metade
de brincadeiras cos pacientes.
Pero isto
é pasarse'
E con tódalas súas forzas lanzou
este peso morto tan lonxe como puido.

E pasou algo
que non comprendeu-
o resto do seu corpo caeu tamén en picado detrás.
Un cambalucho...
Non entendía como estaba conectada
a aquilo que vía por vez primeira.

Foi entón cando a enfermeira lle chiscou un ollo
e lle explicou o que eran.
'Tes unha perna enganchada por aquí
e outra un pouco máis alá.
Unha perna, dúas pernas . . .
Unha e dúas . . .

Agora tes que aprender
como usalas.'

Pregúntome se
nos seguintes meses
o seu corazón foi caendo
igual que caeron pouco a pouco as súas curvaturas,
as curvaturas nas plantas dos pés.

An Mhurúch agus Focail Áirithe
The Mermaid and Certain Words

A serea e algunhas palabras

Fagas o que fagas, xamais lle menciones a palabra
'auga'
nin nada relacionado co mar –
'onda', 'marea', 'océano', 'sonar', 'salitre'.
Ela preferiría ver unha xeada no medio verán
a escoitar historias sobre pesca, barcos, redes de cerca,
trasmallos ou nasas.
Sabe que todo isto existe, por suposto,
e que son importantes
nas vidas doutras persoas.

Pero ela pensa que se tapa os orellas
e xira a ollada en dirección oposta
poderá liberarse por fin
do rincho das
kelpies e demais bestas acuáticas
que proclaman aos catro ventos a súa relación de sangue
durante as horas máis escuras
da noite,
facéndoa arreguizar
e ter suores fríos
ata quedar durmida.

Non ten maior inimigo
ca o recordo da súa propia vida subacuática,
antes de devir enxoita.
Nega con rotundidade
calquera conexión coa auga.
'Nunca tiven ningún interese
nesas supersticións nin nesas tradicións.

O aire puro, o coñecemento, a claridade da ciencia,
esas son as cousas que sempre valorei na miña vida'.

Así e todo
atopei sinais
do seu engano,
pois no Departamento de Folklore Irlandés
da *University College, Dublin*
hai un manuscrito na colección privada
atribuído a ela,
escrito con auga, usando unha aleta de peixe
en papel feito de argazo.

Neste documento poden atoparse trece contos enteiros,
variacións e finais de outros máis coñecido, e tamén
conxuros, rezos, adiviñas e outros textos antigos.
Todo da súa man
pero recitado polo seu pai e a súa avoa.

Sempre nega que exista tal documento,
e as poucas veces que si o admite, di:
'Foi un profesor quen nos mandou facelo como deberes
cando estaba no colexio.
Era obrigatorio'
Preferiría que lle sangrase o nariz un día enteiro
antes que admitir que escribiu todo iso
por vontade propia.

Cuimhne an Uisce
A Recovered Memory of Water

O recordo recuperado do que é a auga

Algunhas veces, mentres a filla da serea
está no baño
cepillando os dentes
ela ten a sensación de que o cuarto
vai, pouco a pouco,
enchéndose de auga.

Comeza polo pés, despois os nocellos,
ata ir subindo máis e máis
polas coxas, a cadeira, a cintura.
E antes de que poida reaccionar
xa lle cubre polo pescozo.
Inclínase para recoller do chan
toallas e farrapos anegados.
Parecen algas,
longos fíos de argazo varados na praia.

Tan rápido como retrocede a auga
o cuarto xa está completamente enxoito outra vez.
Unha sensación terrorífica
que xa é parte do paquete de emocións humanas.
Nunca antes experimentara nada comparable.
Non adquiriu vocabulario suficiente nin axeitado
para poder describir o que lle pasa.
E na súa sesión semanal de terapia
xa ten dabondo do que falar
como para preocuparse de como contarlle á psiquiatra
estes fenómenos estraños.

Non coñece terminoloxía
nin ten puntos de referencia para axudarse.

Tampouco sabe palabras que puidesen
suxerir
o que é a auga.
'É un líquido transparente' di ela, explicándose
con tanta certeza como pode.
'Ben,' di a terapeuta, 'continúa'.
Ela proba de novo.
'Un corpo resplandecente,' di
achegándose cautelosamente á metade da definición
'unha capa finísima, que gotea. Algo húmido.'

Leide Beag
A Tiny Clue

Un pequeno sinal

Terías que pasar toda a vida
escoitando as agachadas
para descubrir o máis mínimo sinal
sobre a orixe da serea. Un día de outono
atopeina
co seu meniño baixo o chal.

"Non es un bebé foca.
Non es un poliño gris de gaivota.
Non es unha lontra acabada de nacer.
Nin tampouco unha cría de balea."

Este era o arrolo que lle cantaba
e que lle deixou de cantar
no momento no que se decatou
de que había alguén preto.

Eu tiven a sensación de que sentía vergoña
de que a tivese escoitado.
E seguín o meu camiño coa impresión
de que aquela cantiga era
un último residuo da súa anterior vida, un forte sabor a mar.

An Mhurúch san Ospidéal
The Mermaid in the Hospital

La sirena en el hospital

Cuando se despertó
encontró en lugar de su cola
un corte limpio
y en la cama junto a ella
dos largos entes
a medio camino entre un cúmulo de algas
y un jamón cocido.

'Sin duda
están de broma.
Debe ser Fin de Año, la mitad de los empleados
estarán ya borrachos,
y la otra mitad
gastando bromas a los pacientes.
Pero esto
es pasarse'
Con todas sus fuerzas lanzó
este peso muerto tan lejos como pudo.

Y pasó algo
que no comprendió-
el resto de su cuerpo siguió la misma trayectoria,
en picado...
No entendía cómo estaba conectada
a esta materia
que acababa de ver por primera vez.

Fue entonces cuando una enfermera le guiño el ojo
y le explicó lo que eran.
'Tienes una pierna conectada por aquí
y otra un poco más allá.

Una pierna, dos piernas . . .
Una y dos . . .
Ahora tienes que aprender
a usarlas.'

Me pregunto si
en los siguientes meses
su corazón cayó
igual que cayeron poco a poco sus curvaturas,
las curvaturas en las plantas de los pies.

An Mhurúch agus Focail Áirithe
  The Mermaid and Certain Words

La sirena y algunas palabras

Hagas lo que hagas, jamás le menciones la palabra
'agua'
ni nada relacionado con el mar –
'olas', 'marea', 'océano', 'sónar', 'salitre'.
Ella preferiría ver una helada en pleno verano
antes que escuchar historias sobre pesca, barcos, redes
    de cerca,
trasmallos o nasas.
Sabe que todo esto existe, por supuesto,
y que son cosas importantes
en la vida de otras personas.

Pero piensa que si se tapas las orejas
y mira hacia otro lado
podrá ser libre por fin
y no volverá a escuchar el relincho de las
kelpies y demás bestias acuáticas
que proclaman su relación de sangre en las horas más
oscuras
de la noche,
provocándole escalofríos
y sudores
hasta quedarse dormida.

No tiene peor enemigo
que el recuerdo de su propia vida bajo las olas
antes de quedarse completamente seca.
Niega con rotundidad
tener cualquier tipo conexión con el agua.
'Nunca me interesaron
esas supersticiones ni esas tradiciones.

El aire fresco, el conocimiento, la claridad de la ciencia,
esas son las cosas que siempre he querido en mi vida'.

Y a pesar de lo que dice,
fui capaz de encontrar señales de su engaño,
ya que en el Departamento de Folklore Irlandés
de la *University College, Dublin*
hay un manuscrito en la colección privada
atribuido a ella,
escrito con agua, usando una aleta de pescado
en papel hecho de sargazo.

En este documento se pueden encontrar trece cuentos
    enteros,
variaciones y finales alternativos de otros, y también
conjuros, rezos, adivinanzas y otros textos antiguos.
Todo de su puño y letra
pero recitado por su padre y su abuela.

Siempre niega que este documento exista,
y las pocas veces que sí lo hace, se excusa:
'Fue un profesor quien nos mandó hacerlo como deberes
cuando estaba en el colegio.
Era obligatorio'
Y preferiría que le sangrase la nariz durante un día entero
antes de admitir que escribió todo eso
por voluntad propia.

Cuimhne an Uisce
A Recovered Memory of Water

El recuerdo recuperado de lo que es el agua

Algunas veces, mientras la hija de la sirena
está en el baño
cepillándose los dientes
ella tiene la sensación de que el cuarto
se empieza a llenar
poco a poco
de agua.

Comienza por los pies, después los tobillos,
hasta ir subiendo
por los muslos, la cadera, la cintura.
Y antes de poder reaccionar
ya le cubre por el cuello.
Se inclina para recoger del suelo
toallas y trapos empapados.
Parecen algas,
largos hilos de sargazo varados en la playa.

Tan rápido como retrocede el agua,
la habitación vuelve a estar totalmente seca.
Una sensación terrorífica
que ya es parte del paquete de emociones humanas.
Nunca había experimentado nada parecido.
No tiene vocabulario suficiente ni adecuado
para poder describir lo que le pasa.
Y en su sesión semanal de terapia
ya tiene mucho de lo que hablar
como para preocuparse de contarle al psiquiatra
estos fenómenos extraños.

No conoce la terminología correcta
ni tiene puntos de referencia para ayudarse.
Tampoco sabe palabras que puedan
sugerir
lo que es el agua.
'Un líquido transparente', dice, explicándose
con tarta certeza como puede.
'Bien,' dice la terapeuta, 'continúa'.
Ella prueba de nuevo.
'Un cuerpo resplandeciente', dice
acercándose cautelosamente a la mitad de su definición
'una capa finísima, que gotea. Algo húmedo.'

Leide Beag
A Tiny Clue

Un pequeño indicio

Tendrías que pasar toda la vida
escuchando a escondidas
para descubrir siquiera un pequeño indicio
sobre el origen de la sirena. Un día de otoño
la encontré
con su bebé bajo el chal.

'No eres un bebé foca azulado.
No eres un pollito gris de gaviota.
No eres una cría de nutria. Ni tampoco
una ballena recién nacida.'

Esta era la nana que le cantaba
y que dejó de cantar
cuando se dio cuenta
de que había alguien cerca.

Yo tuve la sensación de que sentía vergüenza
de que la hubiese escuchado.
Y seguí mi camino con la impresión
de que aquella canción era
un último residuo de su vida anterior, un fuerte sabor a mar.

Translating into German / Deutsch

Reflection by Arndt Wigger

Translating a poem is one way of achieving a better under-standing of the original because one is forced to contem-plate the text more intensely than when simply reading or hearing it. It is often said that poetry cannot be translated, but I maintain that any translation is just an approxima-tion as there can be no complete equivalence on every level of natural language.

Nuala Ní Dhomhnaill has been a beacon for me when it comes to poetry in Irish; I find these works very refresh-ing and worth translating.

Nuala stands out in cultural pluralism, knowing all about differences and shared values, as well as the pains of enforced adaptation which is the theme here. This strange being, presented as a mermaid, taken from maritime folk-lore, is a migrant, confronted with painful cultural clashes, dictated by the dominant powers. That is a scenario not uncommon in present-day Europe. Adaptation, integra-tion, segregation — we are all confronted with this. Perhaps one could have allowed the mermaid to remain as she was, designing a special aquarium for the likes of her — but then . . . Nuala here goes beyond the usual acculturation practices, sarcastically and grotesquely: thematicizing the enforced reshaping of even the body one had lived in.

I translated from the original Irish text, because otherwise too much would have got lost or be contorted. Looking up other translations into other languages would have confused me, apart from being against my own sportive rules. So this is my direct rendering into the language I still know best, German.

These translations are based on the original Irish-language poems.

An Mhurúch san Ospidéal
The Mermaid in the Hospital

Das Meerweib im Spital

Sie erwachte
und ihr Fischschwanz war
nicht mehr da
aber im Bett bei ihr
die zwei langen kalten Dinger.
Man möchte meinen, es seien Schiffstaue
oder Fleischstücke.

‚Das soll ein Scherz sein
bestimmt
am Fress- und Saufabend.
Die halbe Belegschaft ist verrückt
vom Trinken
und die andere Hälfte
sehr zu Späßen aufgelegt.
Wie auch immer, das ist genug,'
und warf die beiden Dinger
aus dem Zimmer hinaus.

Aber dies ist der Teil
den sie nicht versteht
wieso sie hinter ihnen her fiel
'Hals-über-Kopf'.
Was hatten
die beiden Dinger mit ihr zu tun
oder was hatte sie mit denen zu tun?

Die Pflegerin gab ihr den Hinweis
und führte sie der Erkenntnis zu:
‚Dies ist ein Bein, an dich gebunden
und noch eins hier unter dir.

Ein Bein, noch ein Bein,
eins, zwei.
Du musst lernen
mit ihnen zu gehen.'

In den langen Monaten
die folgten
weiß man nicht, ob ihr Herz fiel
so wie die Fußsohle sie drückte,
ihre Fersen ?

An Mhurúch agus Focail Áirithe
The Mermaid and Certain Words

Das Meerweib und die Wörter

Sprich nicht von ‚Wasser' zu ihr
oder über alles was mit dem Meer zu tun hat —
Welle, Gezeiten, Meer, See, Ozean.
Sie mag lieber Sommerfrost als Reden von
Fischfang, Booten, Schlepp- oder Stellnetzen, Hummerkörben.
Sie weiß sehr wohl, dass es solches gibt
und dass andere Leute sich damit zu schaffen machen.

Sie meint, wenn sie die Ohren schließt und den Kopf dreht
könne sie dem widerstehen
und dass sie den strengen Ruf des Seepferdes nicht hört
der ihr ewige Bande kündet tief in der Nacht
mitten in ihrem Schlaf.

Sie hat keinen anderen Feind als zurückzudenken
an das frühere Leben unter Wasser
bevor sie sich wandelte zum neuen Leben auf dem ebenen Land
Sie leugnet rundherum
dass sie je auch nur einen Lausekot damit zu tun hatte
‚Ich mochte diesen Aberglauben nie, auch nicht die Altertümelei.
Luft, Wissen, das klare Licht der Wissenschaft
das begehrte ich.'

Mir gleich, bis ich sie der Lüge überführte.
In der volkskundlichen Bibliothek
sind viele Handschriften der Schulsammlung
von ihrer Hand gekritzelt
mit Wasser geschrieben, mit einem Rochenflügel
auf einem Tangwedel als Pergament.

Dreizehn lange Geschichten
und Teile von anderen, nebst alten Gebeten, Rätseln und
    anderem
sind dort zu finden.
Von ihrem Vater und ihrer alten Mutter nahm sie das
    meiste davon.

Sie verleugnet das glatt: ‚Der Lehrer
hat uns das damals als Hausaufgabe gegeben,
in der Grundschule. Wir mussten es machen.
Wir konnten dem nicht entgehen.'
Eher versprüht sie Nasenblut
bevor sie ihre Herkunft eingesteht.

Cuimhne an Uisce
  A Recovered Memory of Water

Erinnerung an das Wasser

Manchmal wenn ihre Tochter
im Bad ist
ihre Zähne putzt mit einem dicken Büschel
und mit Backpulver
scheint ihr, als füllte sich das Bad mit Wasser.

Es beginnt an den Füßen und Knöcheln
und spritzt immer weiter nach oben
über ihren Hintern und die Hüften
Nicht lange
und es steht ihr bis zu den Knien.
Sie bückt sich öfter und hebt Dinge auf
Tücher und Lappen die sich dort vollsaugen.
Sie sind wie Tang —
die langen Algenfahnen die man
‚Meerfrauhaar‘ nannte oder ‚Fuchsschwanz‘.
Dann plötzlich verschwindet das Wasser
nicht lange
bis der ganze Raum wieder trocken ist.

Große Anstrengung
bringen alle diese Empfindungen.
Letzten Endes hat sie nichts
um das in Einklang zu bringen.
Und kennt überhaupt nicht die richtigen Worte.
Bei der wöchentlichen Therapiesitzung
hat sie große Mühe
diese seltsame Sache zu erklären
und es für den Seelenarzt
richtig auszudrücken.

Sie hat keinen Wortschatz
oder verwandte Begriffe
oder überhaupt ein Wort, das die geringste Ahnung gäbe
was ‚Wasser' ist.
‚Eine durchsichtige Flüssigkeit', sagt sie und gibt sich
   große Mühe.
‚Ja,' sagt der Therapeut, ‚sprich weiter!'
Er lobt sie und bewegt sie zu mehr Spracharbeit.
Sie macht noch einen Versuch.
‚Dünne Masse', nennt sie es,
sorgsam suchend unter den Wörtern.
‚Durchsichtiges Tuch, fließender Stoff, etwas Nasses.'

Leide Beag
  A Tiny Clue

Kleiner Hinweis

Wenn du all dein Leben lang
dem Meerweib lauschen würdest
vielleicht bekämest du ab und an einen Wink
woher sie stammt. Ich traf sie, ganz unerwartet
an einem Herbsttag
ihr Baby unter dem Schal verborgen.

‚Du bist nicht der blaue Vogel der Robbenweibchen,
du bist nicht das graue Küken der Mantelmöwe
du bist nicht das Otterjunge
du bist nicht das Kalb der kahlen Schlanken.

Das sang sie als Schlaflied
aber sie hörte sofort auf
als sie jemand anderen
nahebei bemerkte.

Ich verstand, dass sie sich schämte
dass ich das überhaupt gehört hatte.
Ich verstand auch dass ein kräftiger
Meereshauch aus diesem Schlaflied kam
beim ersten Hören.

Translating into Greek / Ελληνικά

Reflection by Natasha Remoundou/Νατάσα Ρεμούνδου

One navigates through the translation work of Nuala Ní Dhomhnaill's poetry like the mermaids of her verse who must unlearn the permanence of marine life and stand on their new feet. Every stanza, a step, a nautical mile, a breath closer to the surface, and every reading and rereading, the demystification of that feminine lacking of ours, our unbecoming status. And the narrated trauma turns into harbour, oxygen, survival. The translation journey into the Greek language began in 2019 and it can never be completed while Ní Dhomhnaill's mermaid body is still drying up on dry land in an endless search for her lost fishtail. Born from the sea-belly of poetry that springs from the source of the Celtic tongue and the English translations by Paul Muldoon, the plunge into the master aquarium hosting mermaids imagined by genealogies of male writers enacts the first passage of the de-familiarization odyssey. With materials drawn from the heart of chaos, marine fairies, gorgons, sirens, medusas, monsters who sink ships, now gasp for some air space: Homer, John Keats, George Seferis, Pablo Neruda, Costas Karyotakis, Hans Christian Andersen, Alfred Lord Tennyson, T S Eliot, William Butler Yeats, Federico García Lorca, your song waves vibrate from the sea bottom.

By transcribing this underwater nomadic life at a critical distance from inherited traditions in Nuala Ní Dhomhnaill's poetry, I learned to remember flows, storms, surfaces, the silence of the first maternal seabed. And just as words and sounds travel from the wet Irish peat across other mythical oceanographies and geographies, poetry grows gills to breathe at the crossroads of the Atlantic and the Mediterranean. Drowned in seaweed and salt, it is then washed away somewhere between the Ionian Sea and the Aegean. It is July, and the thirst greater than ever.

Many thanks to Professor Rióna Ní Fhrighil, David Howley, and Natasha Merkouri for reading parts of this work while in progress and for their invaluable suggestions.

These translations are based on the English-language translations by Paul Muldoon.

An Mhurúch san Ospidéal
The Mermaid in the Hospital

Η γοργόνα στο νοσοκομείο

Ξύπνησε
κι η ψαροουρά της
φευγάτη
μα στο κρεβάτι δίπλα της
ήταν δυο μακριά, κρύα αποτέτοια.
Θαρρείς πως ήταν κουβάρια από κέλπιες
ή κομμάτια κρέας.

'Χωρίς καμία αμφιβολία
αστειεύονται,
παραμονή Πρωτοχρονιάς.
Το μισό προσωπικό
τύφλα στο μεθύσι
και τ'άλλο μισό κάνει πλάκες.
Όμως, αυτό παραπάει.'
Κι εκτόξευσε έτσι τα δυο αποτέτοια έξω απ'το δωμάτιο.

Αλλά να που
ακόμα δεν μπορεί να καταλάβει-
γιατί εκείνη κατρακύλησε μαζί τους...
Πώς συνδεόταν
μ'εκείνα τ'αποτέτοια
και πώς εκείνα συνδέονταν μ'αυτήν.

Χάρη στη νοσοκόμα που της έκανε νόημα
έμαθε τα καθέκαστα.
' Έχεις ένα πόδι προσκολλημένο εκεί πάνω
κι άλλο ένα κάτω απ'αυτό.
Ένα πόδι, δύο πόδια . . .
Έν' δυο . . .

Τώρα πρέπει να μάθεις
τι μπορούν να κάνουν.'

Στους μήνες
που ακολούθησαν,
αναρωτιέμαι αν βούλιαξε η καρδιά της
όπως πέσανε οι καμάρες των ποδιών της,
οι εσωτερικοί ταρσοί της.

An Mhurúch agus Focail Áirithe
The Mermaid and Certain Words

Η γοργόνα και κάποιες λέξεις

Ό,τι κι αν κάνεις μην αναφέρεις ποτέ τη λέξη
'νερό'
ή οτιδήποτε άλλο θυμίζει θάλασσα-
'κύμα', 'παλίρροια', 'ωκεανός', 'πέλαγος', 'αρμύρα'.
Θα προτιμούσε να φανταστεί την άφιξη του παγετού
καταμεσής του καλοκαιριού
παρά ν'ακούει για ψαρέματα, βάρκες, τράτες ή δίχτυα,
κι αστακοδοχεία.
Το ξέρει πως τέτοια πράγματα υπάρχουν, φυσικά,
και πως άλλοι
με τέτοια έχουν παρτίδες.

Νομίζει πως αν κλείσει τ'αυτιά της και
γυρίσει το κεφάλι της αλλού
θα γλυτώσει απ'αυτά
και δεν θα ξανακούσει ποτέ το δυνατό χλιμίντρισμα
του υδρόβιου πνεύματος ή του ιππόκαμπου
να διεκδικούν τη συγγένειά της εξ αίματος την πιο
   σκοτεινή
ώρα της νύχτας,
προκαλώντας της ένα ξέσπασμα ανατριχίλας και
τον ιδρώτα να τη μαστιγώνει
όταν την παίρνει ο ύπνος.

Τίποτα δεν μισεί πιο πολύ
απ'το να της υπενθυμίζουν την υποβρύχια ζωή της
πριν γυρίσει σελίδα σε στεγνή στεριά.
Αρνείται σθεναρά
πως είχε την παραμικρή σχέση ποτέ μ'αυτήν.
'Ποτέ δεν μ'ενδιέφεραν
εκείνες οι παλιές προκαταλήψεις ή οι παλιές παραδόσεις.

96

Καθαρό αέρα, γνώση, τη λαμπερή ευφυΐα της
επιστήμης
ήταν τα μόνα που λαχτάρησα.'

Δεν θα με πείραζε ούτως ή άλλως αλλά εγώ η ίδια
την αποκάλυψα πάνω στην απάτη.
Στο Τμήμα Ιρλανδικής Λαογραφίας
στο Πανεπιστήμιο του Δουβλίνου,
υπάρχει ένα ολόκληρο χειρόγραφο στη Συλλογή της
Σχολής
που καταγράφηκε από 'κείνη,
γραμμένο στο νερό, με σαλαχιού πτερύγιο για
    στυλογράφο,
σ' ένα μακρύ πάπυρο από κέλπιες.

Μέσα εκεί βρίσκονται δεκατρία μεγάλα παραμύθια
και άλλα ψιλολόγια, μαζί με
φυλαχτά, παλιές προσευχές, γρίφους και τέτοια.
Απ' τον πατέρα της και τη γιαγιά της πιο πολύ
τα κατέγραψε.

Αρνείται να παραδεχτεί την ύπαρξή του, κι όταν
το κάνει,
'Ήταν ο δάσκαλος που μας το΄δωσε εργασία για το σπίτι,
πριν χρόνια στο δημοτικό.
'Έπρεπε να το κάνουμε.'
Θα προτιμούσε να υποστεί βαριά ρινορραγία
παρά να παραδεχτεί πως έβαλε το χέρι της
στη σύνθεσή του.

Cuimhne an Uisce
A Recovered Memory of Water

Μια ανάμνηση νερού

Συχνά όταν η κόρη της γοργόνας
είναι στο μπάνιο
καθαρίζοντας τα δόντια της με μια χοντρή βούρτσα
και μαγειρική σόδα
εκείνη έχει την αίσθηση πως το δωμάτιο γεμίζει
νερό.

Ξεκινά απ' τα πόδια και τους αστραγάλους της
και γλιστράει όλο και πιο ψηλά
πάνω απ' τους μηρούς και τους γοφούς και τη μέση.
Σε χρόνο μηδέν
φτάνει ψηλά στις μασχάλες της.
Σκύβει μέσα να μαζέψει
πετσέτες χεριών και προσώπου και όλ' αυτά
που είναι μουλιασμένα.
Όλα μοιάζουν με φύκια-
όπως εκείνες οι μακριές τούφες από κέλπιες που
τις αποκαλούσαν
'μαλλιά γοργόνας' ή 'άγανο'.
Τότε ξαφνικά το νερό υποχωρεί
και σε χρόνο μηδέν
το δωμάτιο είναι εντελώς στεγνό και πάλι.

Μια απαίσια αίσθηση πίεσης
είναι αναπόσπαστο κομμάτι αυτών των συναισθημάτων.
Στο κάτω-κάτω δεν μπορεί
να το συγκρίνει με τίποτ' άλλο.
Δεν έχει το λεξιλόγιο για τίποτα απ' όλα αυτά.
Κάθε εβδομάδα στις θεραπευτικές συνεδρίες
έχει περισσότερα απ' όσα χρειάζεται να πει

μόνο και μόνο για να περιγράψει αυτό το παράξενο
φαινόμενο
και να το εκφράσει όπως πρέπει
στον ψυχίατρο.

Δεν έχει την ορολογία
ούτε τα σημεία αναφοράς
ή καμία απολύτως λέξη που θα αποτελούσε την
παραμικρή
ένδειξη
για το τι θα μπορούσε να είναι το νερό.
''Ενα διάφανο υγρό', λέει, βάζοντας τα δυνατά της.
'Μάλιστα', λέει ο θεραπευτής, 'συνέχισε'.
Την καλοπιάνει και την καταφέρνει να πλάσει λέξεις.
Εκείνη κάνει ακόμα μια προσπάθεια.
'Μια λεπτή ροή', το αποκαλεί εκείνη,
ανιχνεύοντας επιφυλακτικά ανάμεσα στις λέξεις.
'Μια λαμπερή μεμβράνη. Που στάζει διάφορα. Κάτι υγρό.'

Leide Beag
A Tiny Clue

Μια μικροσκοπική ένδειξη

Θα μπορούσες να περάσεις ολόκληρη τη ζωή σου
κρυφακούγοντας τη γοργόνα
προτού εντοπίσεις την παραμικρή ένδειξη
για την πραγματική καταγωγή της. Μια φθινοπωρινή
    μέρα
την συνάντησα τυχαία με το παιδί της
ενώ το παρηγορούσε κάτω από το σάλι της.

'Δεν είσαι το γαλαζοπράσινο μωρό της φώκιας.
Δεν είσαι το γκρίζο κλωσσόπουλο του γιγαντόγλαρου.
Δεν είσαι το μικρό της βύδρας. Ούτε είσαι
το μοσχάρι της λεπτής άκερης αγελάδας.'

Αυτό ήταν το νανούρισμα που τραγουδούσε
αλλά το διέκοψε απότομα
αμέσως αντιλήφθηκε
πως κάποιος άλλος ήταν στη γειτονιά.

Είχα μιαν ευδιάκριτη αίσθηση πως ντράπηκε
κατ'αρχάς που την είχα ακούσει.
Κι επίσης αποχώρησα με την εντύπωση
πως το νανούρισμα θύμιζε τουλάχιστον θάλασσα.

County Mayo-Athens, 2019-2021

Translating into Japanese / 日本語

Reflection by Mitsuko Ohno

My first encounter with Nuala Ní Dhomhnaill's poetry was in 1990, when a copy, possibly the first one brought into Japan, of *Pharaoh's Daughter* (The Gallery Press, 1990) was given to me as a gift from my Irish-American mentor. It contained Irish poems written by a female poet unknown in Japan, with English translations by more familiar poets. It turned out to be an electrifying encounter, because as soon as I finished reading the first poem 'Geasa' ('The Bond'), I was spellbound by the enigma it posed.

Ní Dhomhnaill, re-collecting voices from Irish myth and folklore, and recounting them in a subversive mode by mixing in humour and eroticism, appealed to me as an exceptionally intelligent modern-day woman trying to fight against the male-centred institution/tradition. I could hear her distinct voice calling to me through the English tongue of her translators.

Striving myself at that time to establish Irish Literature and incorporate Women's Studies in my English Department's curriculum, I saw immediately that *Pharaoh's Daughter* could go beyond my personal fascination, and offer resourceful material for education also. Contemporary issues in her poems were familiar to women in Japan and when I tried them out with young women in my seminar they showed a very positive reaction. Very soon I decided to translate Nuala's poems and publish for general readers beyond the academic world.

A decade later Ní Dhomhnaill and I first met in Dublin and, after her two trips to Japan, the new collection of her poems, titled *Pharaoh-no-musume* (*Pharaoh's Daughter*), was published by Shichosha in Tokyo in 2001. Nuala's generous support by offering unpublished poems with English cribs and ample time for my questions and our discussions made this project possible. The collection contains Irish and Japanese poems, with notes, essays, elucidations and her interview in Japanese and in English. The accompanying CD contains recordings in Irish and in Japanese giving readers a taste of a poetry reading.

The collection took on a life of its own, with readers responding in various ways. After the launch a woman came to Nuala to say, 'To know that you live and write such poems makes this world worth living in, and for that I thank you.' A visual artist, Miho Ohtsubo, who was inspired by the poems, requested my permission to quote them at her exhibitions, and a musician, Chikuzan Takahashi II, turned the poems into new folk songs. These are artists with whom I have been collaborating since and they convinced me that, among diversely gendered and classed voices in our language, my choice of this lucid woman's voice was right, because Nuala's focus on human sufferings inspired them acutely as women to express their empathy beyond the language and form.

These translations are based on the English-language translations by Paul Muldoon and follow direct engagement with Nuala Ní Dhomhnaill regarding the original Irish-language texts.

An Mhurúch san Ospidéal
   The Mermaid in the Hospital

病院の人魚

彼女は 目を覚ます
人魚の尻尾は
もう 無くなっている
ベッドの中にあるのは
二つの 長くて 冷たいモノ
まるで もつれた幅広の昆布
あるいは うす切りにされた肉片

「あの人たち 頭が
変になったにちがいない
どんちゃん騒ぎの大晦日
職員の半分は 酔っ払い
残る半分も
悪ふざけばかり
でも たとえ そうだとしても
これは やり過ぎ」
そういって 彼女は放り投げた
二つのモノを 病室の外へ

だが それから先が
彼女にはわからないーー
モノたちに続いて 彼女まで

ひっくり返って ベッドの下
いったい どう繋がっている
彼女と あの二つのモノ
どんな関係
それらと 彼女

看護婦が 身振り手振りで
教えてくれた ことの真相
「この あなたに繋がれたモノは 足
そこの もう一つも 足
足 一本 もう一本・・・
一歩 歩いて もう一歩・・・
あなたは 習わなくてはいけないの
どうやって 足で歩くのか」

その後
長い月日が過ぎた
誰も 知らない
足の裏が平たくなり
土踏まずが 消えてしまったように
彼女の希望も 沈んでしまったのだろうか

An Mhurúch agus Focail Áirithe
The Mermaid and Certain Words

人魚と忌み言葉

とにかく 「水」という言葉は口にしないで
ほかに 海を思わせる言葉もだめーー
「波」 「潮」 「外洋」 「荒れる沖」 「塩水」
釣りや船 引き網やトランメル網 海老壺の話を聞かされるより
真夏に降りる霜の心配をするほうが ずっとまし
もちろん彼女も知っている そんなものがあることも
それにかかわるのが仕事の
人たちだっていることも

彼女は思っている 耳をふさぎ 顔をそむけさえすれば
すっかり自由になれると
もう二度と聞こえないはず ケルピーや海馬のいななきも
深い闇の中から 血縁をうったえる
そのかん高い声は ぐっすり眠る彼女の
全身を鳥肌立て 冷や汗を吹きださせる

彼女が この世でいちばん忌みきらうのは
思い出させられること 水の中での昔の暮らし
陸に移り住むよりも 前のこと
彼女は あくまでも否定する
これまで どんなかかわりも
持ったことがないと 「興味なかったわ

古くさい迷信や かび臭い風習なんて
新鮮な空気 学問知識 科学の明るい光
わたしが夢中になったのは それだけよ」

どうでもいいことだけど
わたしは 気付いてしまった
彼女が嘘をついていると
ダブリン大学
アイルランド民俗学科の
資料室に収められている
エイのヒレ骨をペン代わりに
水のインクで 長い昆布の巻紙に書かれた
彼女の筆跡の文書

中には 十三の長い物語
それに あれこれの話の寄せ集め
呪文や 古い祈りの言葉に なぞなぞの類
ほとんどは 父親と祖母から
聞きとって 書いたもの

その存在すら認めたくない彼女の しぶしぶの弁明
「校長先生が
宿題で書かせたの
むかし 国民小学校時代のことよ
いやでも 書かなければいけなかった」

自分で書いたと認めるくらいなら 彼女には
ひどい鼻血で苦しむ方が ずっとまし

Cuimhne an Uisce
A Recovered Memory of Water

よみがえる水の記憶

ときどき バスルームで
目の細かいブラシと重曹で
歯を磨いている人魚の娘が
ふと感じる 部屋を満たしていく
水

まず足もとへ それから足首
水は 上へ 上へ
太ももからお尻 さらには腰へ
瞬く間に
脇の下まで届く
腰を曲げ 水の中に手を伸ばすと
手ぬぐいやタオルやらの
布は ぐしょ濡れで
海の中の 藻のように見える――
長くて細い昆布の糸 昔は「人魚の髪」とか
「エノコログサ」と呼ばれていた 海藻のよう
突然また 水は 引いていく
そして 瞬く間に
部屋は もう乾ききっている

強度の不安が
こんなときの つきもの
結局のところ 彼女には わからない
他の 何に例えればよいのか
それらをあらわす語彙すら 持っていない
毎週の治療面談で
この奇妙な現象を説明するだけでも
精一杯
精神科の医者が
期待する表現なぞ とうてい無理

彼女は そもそも専門用語なんて 知らない
基準となるものが わからない
水とは いったい何なのか
それをあらわす手がかりすらもない
「透けてみえる液」というのが 精一杯
「いいね」と医師 「続けて」とおだてて
そそのかす言葉創り
もう一度 彼女は試してみる
「かすかな流れ」と 口に出し
こわごわ 言葉の群れに投げ入れる
「つやのある膜 ポタポタ滴る 湿ったモノ」

Leide Beag
  A Tiny Clue

ささやかな手がかり

人魚の話すのを 一生かけて
立ち聞きしても
彼女が ほんとうは どこからやってきたのか
手がかりを掴むのすら むつかしい
ある秋の日 偶然 わたしは
人魚と子どもに出くわした
ショールにくるんだ赤ん坊を あやしているところ

「おまえは 青色の子アザラシ じゃない
オオセグロカモメの 灰色のひな でもない
カワウソの子ども でもないし
ほっそりイルカの赤ちゃん でもないよ」

これが 彼女の口ずさんでいた子守唄
でも 途中で やめてしまった
すぐに気づいたのだ
誰かが近くにいることに

はっきり感じとれたのは なにより
立ち聞きされて 恥ずかしかったこと
それに 子守唄からただよってくる
紛れもない 海の匂い

Translating into Polish / Polski

Reflection by Jerzy Jarniewicz

My first encounter with Nuala Ní Dhomhnaill's poetry was in 1992 when an Irish friend of mine, Cathal McCabe, presented me with a copy of *Pharaoh's Daughter* (The Gallery Press, 1990). I felt immediately attracted to these poems which were so different from what Polish poetry, dominated at that time by male voices, looked like. They are often intimate and private, but address also public issues, break social taboos and challenge received ideas. Though anchored in things recognizably Irish, they are amazingly communicable. The clarity of Nuala's writing goes in hand with a certain enigmatic tone: a premonition of things which cannot be captured in language, yet haunt her poems. The use of myths, folklore or history does not stop them from sounding very contemporary, as Nuala's forays into the past are in fact journeys through the world of today.

In 1997, with Cathal's assistance, I invited Nuala to take part in one of the Poetry Seminars which I had been organizing in Łódź for over ten years. As her visit proved a success she came again to participate in our event in 2003. In 2014 she visited Warsaw where she gave a reading at the Museum of Literature and promoted the anthology *Sześć Poetek Irlandzkich* (*Six Irish Women Poets*, Biuro Literackie, 2012), which included a selection of her poems with my translations. Six years later Nuala was awarded the prestigious Zbigniew Herbert Prize.

Translating Nuala's poetry into Polish was a rewarding experience. What I found particularly challenging was her use of various registers for which I had to find Polish equivalents: the poem 'Cuimhne an Uisce' ('A Recovered Memory of Water') has the flow of a fairy tale, but uses a matter-of-fact diction, with prosaic, even technical vocabulary and, on top of that, creative, imaginative phrases which so memorably conclude the poem. Other difficulties I had to face were related to the fact that Polish is a gendered language. 'Mermaid' and 'water', for example, are both 'she', which might be confusing for the reader, so I had to replace two pronouns with a noun. And, finally, I tried to do my best to convey a sense of the subtle, unobtrusive humour which makes this poem of Nuala's so appealing.

This translation is based on the English-language translation by Paul Muldoon and follows direct engagement with Nuala Ní Dhomhnaill regarding the original Irish-language texts. It was originally published in my book *Sześć Poetek Irlandzkich* (*Six Irish Women Poets*).

Cuimhne an Uisce
A Recovered Memory of Water

Odzyskana pamięć wody

Kiedy córka syreny
zamyka się w łazience i
szoruje zęby grubą szczoteczką
i sodą kuchenną,
ma czasem wrażenie, że łazienka
napełnia się wodą.

Czuje, jak woda wzbiera u jej stop i kostek,
jak podnosi się coraz wyżej
do ud, bioder i pasa.
Ani się obejrzy,
a woda sięga jej po pachy.
Schyla się, by podnieść
ręcznik, ściereczkę, inne drobne rzeczy,
już całkiem mokre.
Wyglądają jak glony,
jak pasma wodorostów, zwane ongiś
„syrenim włosiem" albo „lisią kitą".
Woda jednak szybko ustępuje
i w okamgnieniu
łazienka znów jest sucha.

Doznaniom syrenki towarzyszy
potworne napięcie.
Pod koniec dnia nie ma już nic,
do czego mogłaby je porównać.
Brak jej odpowiedniego słownika.
Na cotygodniowej terapii
ma zbyt wiele problemów na głowie,
by opisać to niecodzienne zjawisko

i opowiedzieć o nim składnie
psychoterapeucie.

Brak jej terminologii,
brak punktów odniesienia,
brak słów, które określiłyby trafnie,
czym jest woda.
„Płyn przezroczysty", mówi, bardzo się starając.
„Dobrze", odpowiada terapeuta, „Dobrze, mów dalej".
I kusi ją, namawia do słowotwórstwa.
Córka syreny próbuje raz jeszcze.
„Szklisty nurt", chce rzecz nazwać,
myszkując ostrożnie wśród słów.
„Lśniąca powłoka. Mokrość. Coś bardzo wilgotnego".

Translating into Polish / Polski

Reflection by Magdalena Kleszczewska

I first heard Nuala Ní Dhomhnaill read her poems in Warsaw back in 2014. Although I had been familiar with her poetry before, its boldness and carnality (somewhat reminiscent of the Polish poet Marta Podgórnik) seemed all the more vivid in Irish. Or so it sounded that evening. Six years later I took on the task of translating three poems from the merfolk sequence. For me this was not simply a translation exercise but a very personal engagement. With my love of Nuala Ní Dhomhnaill's poetry I have sought to get to the heart of each poem, bringing an insight to the images evoked in them.

The challenges were both linguistic and aesthetic. Collocations are one thing, but when the poetry's main feature is the rhythm and the beat of words, how does one pace a poem if one is not able to read the original text aloud? I had no choice but to trust Paul Muldoon's English translations.

Following the advice given by my fellow translator Jakub Głuszak, I decided to translate the sequence under the title 'Udomowieni Muruchowie', which borrows directly from the Irish, and may be back-translated as 'Domesticated merfolk' or 'Na murúcha ceansaithe'. By simple inflection 'na murúcha' have once again been assimilated — this time into the Polish language. Yet it was their story that inspired me to take an Irish-language course.

Turning to Irish allowed me an attempt, if only of a phonetic kind, at a semi-macaronic equivalence of the 'cocs-um-bo-head' phrase (quite an offensive one). I was also given a once-in-a-lifetime chance to be the nurse reciting a Polish version of the 'cos, cos eile' nursery rhyme. Although not all the original richness could be reproduced, not all is lost, I believe.

These translations are based on the English-language

translations by Paul Muldoon and refer to the original Irish-language versions also.

An Mhurúch san Ospidéal
The Mermaid in the Hospital

Syrena w szpitalu

Kiedy się obudziła, odkryła,
że jej rybi ogon
zniknął bez śladu,
ale w łóżku leżały
dwa długie, zimne dzyndzle.
Wyglądały jak pasma glonów
lub kawałki szynki.

„Jak nic
robią sobie jaja,
w końcu jest sylwester.
Połowa personelu pijana jak bela,
procenty ścięły ich z nóg,
a druga połowa
stroi sobie żarty.
Jak by nie było,
to już jest przegięcie".
Z tą myślą prasnęła
dwoma dzyndzlami za drzwi.

No i właśnie tego
nie może pojąć:
czemu za nimi poleciała
i runęła dupą-na-łeb . . .
Co ją łączyło
z dwoma dzyndzlami
i jaki związek one miały
z nią?

Pielęgniarka mrugnęła do niej
porozumiewawczo.

„Tu masz doczepioną jedną nogę,
a z tej strony drugą.
Dwa kolana, nogi dwie,
wszystko pięknie zgadza się.
Prawa nóżka, lewa nóżka,
zacznij chodzić jak kaczuszka".

Ciekawe, czy przez te długie miesiące,
które potem nastały
jej serce się ugięło
podobnie jak łuk,
łuk jej podbicia.

An Mhurúch agus Focail Áirithe
The Mermaid and Certain Words

Syrena i pewne słowa

Pod żadnym pozorem nie wspominaj jej o słowie „woda"
ani o żadnym innym, które trąci morzem —
„fala", „ocean", „przypływ", „kipiel", „toń".
Woli już mróz, który chwycił w lecie niż wzmianki
o połowach, łodziach, włokach albo drygach, klatkach na
    homary.
Wie o ich istnieniu, naturalnie.
Wie, że inni ludzie
miewają z nimi do czynienia.

Sądzi, że jeśli zakryje uszy i odwróci głowę,
uwolni się od nich
i już nigdy nie usłyszy głośnego rżenia kelpie,
który w otchłani nocy, we śnie twardym jak kamień
wypomina łączące ich więzy krwi,
sprowadzając na nią gęsią skórkę oraz zlewne poty.

Nie ma dla niej nic gorszego
niż te aluzje do podwodnego życia,
które wiodła,
nim rozpoczęła nowy rozdział na suchym lądzie.
Stanowczo zaprzecza,
że kiedykolwiek
miała coś wspólnego
z tamtym światem. „Nie obchodziły mnie nigdy
ani żadne zabobony, ani dawne tradycje.

Świeże powietrze, wiedza i blask nauki
— to wszystko, czego zawsze pragnęłam".

Mnie tam by było wszystko jedno, tyle że
to właśnie ja
odkryłam jej konfabulacje.
Na Uniwersytecie Dublińskim
w Kolekcji Szkolnej
Wydziału Irlandzkiego Folkloru
znajduje się zbiór manuskryptów
wykonanych przez nią.
Spisała je w wodzie,
na długim zwoju listownicy,
płetwą płaszczki służącą za pióro.

Składa się z trzynastu długich opowieści,
skrawków różnych historii, a także
zaklęć, dawnych modlitw, zagadek i takich tam.
Przekazanych jej przez ojca i babkę
w głównej mierze.

Zaprzecza ich istnieniu, tłumacząc się pokrętnie:
„Nauczyciel zadał nam to jako pracę domową,
w podstawówce — wieki temu.
Musieliśmy to zrobić. Nie mieliśmy wyboru".
Prędzej jej krew bryźnie z nosa
niż się przyzna, że przyłożyła do tego płetwę.

Leide Beag
A Tiny Clue

Znikomy trop

Można spędzić całe życie,
podsłuchując syrenę,
nim trafi się na znikomy trop,
wskazujący na to, skąd rzeczywiście pochodzi.
Pewnego jesiennego dnia
natknęłam się na nią i jej dziecko,
gdy próbowała utulić je pod chustą.

„Nie jesteś turkusowym szczenięciem foki.
Ni szarym pisklęciem mewy siodłatej.
Nie jesteś oseskiem wydry. Ani cielątkiem
smukłej bezrogiej krowy".

Taką oto nuciła kołysankę,
lecz przerwała raptownie.
Z miejsca zdała sobie sprawę,
że ktoś jest w pobliżu.

Miałam poczucie, że przede wszystkim
spłoszyłam ją swym wsłuchiwaniem się.
Miałam też nieodparte wrażenie,
że kołysanka, mówiąc delikatnie, trąci morzem.

Translating into Polish / Polski

Reflection by Barbara Szot

I like stories. I have always been a prose reader by preference because I expected prose to be better at telling stories than modern-day poetry. I now feel that Nuala Ní Dhomhnaill proved me wrong. It was the narrative so cleverly woven together that attracted me to the poem 'An Mhurúch sa Ospidéal' ('The Mermaid in the Hospital'), so minimalistic in the sheer number of words used and yet so robust.

My first encounter with the poem was at the roundtable session on the Aistriú project at the 2019 EFACIS conference in Ljubljana. My reading was thus immediately informed by the presentation and the discussion that followed. Somebody there noted that the lines 'Cos, cos eile, / a haon, a dó. / Caithfidh tú foghlaim / conas siúl leo.' sounded like a nursery rhyme which is something I tried to recreate in my translation for that fragment. It was never just me and the poem. From the outset I was navigating between other people's readings and learning from them.

My work started with the original Irish text (with Radvan Markus's kind assistance), but it was not until I studied the translations by Paul Muldoon and Medbh McGuckian that I began to figure out my own approach to the poem and in the finishing stages Magdalena Kleszczewska's rendition helped me make some final decisions. Muldoon's play with words was particularly inspiring in many ways. I largely followed his example, but on occasions his choices also highlighted things that I felt I wanted done differently. His 'legless with drink' together with 'thingammies' made me think that the second stanza is too early in the poem for leg-related vocabulary to be used. I tried to keep my puns watery and marine to be in line with the mermaid's perspective and only moved on to legs and walking in the later stanzas.

This translation is based on the original Irish-language

poem with reference to Paul Muldoon's English-language translation.

An Mhurúch san Ospidéal
The Mermaid in the Hospital

Syrena w szpitalu

Obudziła się,
a jej ogona nie było,
za to w łóżku leżały z nią
dwie długie, zimne rzeczy.
Można by wziąć je za źdźbła morskiej trawy
albo za dwie porcje mięsa.

„To jakiś kawał,
niewątpliwie,
sylwestrowe szaleństwo.
Część towarzystwa całkiem zalana,
reszta ma przypływ
ochoty na żarty.
Tak czy owak, to już przesada"
i z myślą tą obie rzeczy
cisnęła za drzwi.

Jednego jednak
nie mogła pojąć —
że i ona poleciała wtedy
na łeb, na tyłek.
Jak związane
były z nią te rzeczy
i jaki związek z nimi dwiema
miała ona?

Uświadomiła ją pielęgniarka,
pomogła dojść, co jest czym.
„To tu, to jest, proszę pani, noga,
a tam pod spodem ma pani drugą.
Prawa, lewa,
raz i dwa.

Teraz pani chodzić ma".

Czy podczas długich miesięcy,
które potem nadeszły,
jej serce podążyło
w ślad za jej stopami?

Translating into Portuguese / Português

Reflection by Maria Filomena Louro who supported the translators (Hugo Sousa, Carolina Carvalho and Luís Ramos)

Many of us have had people in our families who came over forty years ago from the former Portuguese colonies and had to adapt to a very different environment. They felt like fish out of water, to use what is also a Portuguese expression. These poems can begin to express that situation, even if they were not about this specific group or their situation. This sense of alienation can be felt by anyone; displacement is present in all of our societies.

In translating these poems this group of student translators was challenged to find the adequate vocabulary to evoke water imagery and needed to research Irish society and history, not a core subject for them. Portugal being a country with one of the largest maritime areas in Europe should imply a close contact with the sea and its professions and crafts. However, references to fishing artefacts which would immediately evoke a sense of daily contact with the sea, a common shared experience of humans and merfolk, was the object of specific research. Socially this is a permanently shrinking community. Another challenge was to find the right note to refer to body parts without sounding rude or scientific, a difficult balance to establish.

This exercise of translating for the Aistriú project made this group of students reflect on the issue of displacement, the pain and fear, as well as the hope when leaving one's native context. It also inspired them to reflect on the difficulties of adapting to the new environment, often feeling like an amputation as in these poems

Carolina Carvalho, Hugo Sousa and Luís Ramos engaged in this project as part of their Literary Translation work in the first year of the Masters in Translation and Multilingual Communication, at Minho University, Portugal. The translations were done individually and discussed by the collective in the classroom. The final revision was completed by the tutor who selected their work for Aistriú; it was independently revised by our colleague and translator Ana Maria Chaves, whom we acknowledge and thank for her collaboration.

These translations are based on the English-language translations by Paul Muldoon.

An Mhurúch san Ospidéal
The Mermaid in the Hospital

A Sereia no Hospital

Ela acordou
e viu que a cauda
tinha desaparecido
mas que com ela na cama
estavam dois longos e frios empecilhos.
Podia até confundi-los com algas entrelaçadas
ou fatias de presunto.

"Estão, sem dúvida,
a gozar comigo
por ser véspera de Ano Novo.
Metade do pessoal sem pernas
a cair de bêbedo
e a outra metade
a pregar partidas.
Mas isto já é brincadeira
a mais."
E, dizendo isso, lançou
os dois empecilhos para fora do quarto.

Mas isto é o que
ela ainda não percebeu —
porque foi de roldão atrás deles
e ficou de rabo para o ar . . .
como estava ela ligada
aos dois empecilhos
e como estavam eles ligados
a ela.

Foi a enfermeira que lhe deu uma pista
e lhe explicou tudo.

"Tens uma perna presa a ti aqui
e outra por baixo dessa.
Uma perna, duas pernas . . .
Uma, duas . . .
Agora tens de aprender
o que elas podem fazer."

Nos longos meses
que se seguiram,
Será que o seu coração caía
tal qual as plantas caíam,
as plantas dos pés.

An Mhurúch agus Focail Áirithe
The Mermaid and Certain Words

A Sereia e Certas Palavras

Faças o que fizeres nunca menciones a palavra 'água'
ou qualquer outra coisa que cheire o mar —
'onda', maré', 'oceano', 'as tempestades marinhas', 'a
salmoura'.
Mais depressa ela contemplaria a chegada de geada em
    pleno verão
do que ouvir histórias de pesca, barcos, arrastões ou
    tresmalhos, armadilhas para lagostas.
Sabe da existência dessas, claro,
e que outras pessoas
lidam com elas.

Acha que se tapar os ouvidos e virar a cabeça
se verá livre delas
e nunca mais terá de ouvir os relinchos dos hipocampos
    ou cavalos marinhos
a reclamarem o seu parentesco com ela à hora mais tétrica
    da noite,
pondo-a com pele de galinha e profusos suores a escorrer
enquanto dorme profundamente.

Não há nada que mais deteste
do que relembrarem-lhe a vida subaquática que levou
até começar vida nova em terra
Nega completamente
alguma vez ter tido qualquer tipo de associação
com ela. 'Nunca tive interesse algum
nessas velhas superstições, ou em qualquer das velhas
    tradições.
Ar fresco, conhecimento, a luz irradiante da ciência
são tudo o que alguma vez desejei.'

Para mim tanto faz de uma maneira ou de outra, mas eu
   mesma
lhe descobri
a mentira.
No Departamento de Folclore Irlandês
no University College, em Dublin,
há um manuscrito nos arquivos da biblioteca
que foi redigido por ela,
escrito a água, com a barbatana de uma raia como caneta,
num longo rolo de algas.

Nele se encontram treze longas histórias
e trechos e fragmentos de outras, juntamente com
encantamentos, velhas orações, adivinhas e coisas do género.
Foi do seu pai e da avó, na sua maioria,
que as recolheu.

Recusa-se a aceitar a sua existência, e, quando o faz,
'Foi o professor que nos deu isso como trabalho de casa,
no secundário.
Tínhamos de o fazer.'
Preferia que lhe batessem
a admitir alguma vez se ter envolvido na sua composição.

Cuimhne an Uisce
A Recovered Memory of Water

Uma Memória de Água Recuperada

Às vezes quando a filha da sereia
está na casa de banho
a lavar os dentes com uma escova espessa
e bicarbonato de sódio
tem a sensação de que o quarto se está a encher
de água.

Começa por lhe chegar aos pés e tornozelos
e vai subindo progressivamente
até às coxas, ancas e cintura.
Num abrir e fechar de olhos
já lhe dá pelas axilas
Ela baixa-se dentro de água para pegar
nas toalhas de rosto, toalhetes e todas essas coisas
que estão encharcadas no fundo.
Estão todas com ar de moliço —
como as longas algas a que outrora se chamava
'cabelo de sereia' ou 'erva-de-febra'.
Mas assm como chegou a água desce
e num abrir e fechar de olhos
o quarto fica completamente seco de novo.

Uma terrível sensação de stress
acompanha estas emoções.
Bem vistas as coisas, ela afinal não tem mais nada
a que a comparar.
Não tem vocabulário para nada disso.
Na sua sessão de terapia semanal
tem mais do que o suficiente
para descrever este fenómeno estranho

e para o reportar devidamente
ao seu psiquiatra.

Não tem a terminologia
ou quaisquer pontos de referência
ou uma única palavra que possa dar a mínima sugestão
sobre o que a água poderia ser.
'Um líquido transparente', diz ela, dando o seu melhor.
'Sim', diz o terapeuta, 'continua'.
Ele persuade-a e incentiva-a a formar palavras.
Ela tenta de novo.
'Um fluxo fino', chama-lhe ela,
procurando com cuidado a palavra certa.
'Uma camada reluzente. Algo que pinga. Algo molhado'.

Leide Beag
A Tiny Clue

Uma Pequena Pista

Poderias passar a vida inteira
a escutar a sereia
sem encontrares uma única pista
sobre a sua verdadeira origem. Um dia de outono
encontrei-a por acaso
a ela e ao seu rebento
enquanto o confortava debaixo do xaile.

'Tu não és a cria verde-azulada da foca.
Tu não és o pintainho cinzento do gaivotão-real.
Tu não és o bebé da lontra. Nem és
o bezerro da esbelta vaca sem chifres.'

Era esta a canção de embalar que cantava
Mas de súbito parou
assim que percebeu
que estava mais alguém por perto.

Tive a nítida sensação de que sentiu vergonha
sobretudo de eu a ter ouvido.
Também fiquei com a impressão de que
a canção, no mínimo, emanava fragrâncias a mar.

Acknowledgements

The Multilingual Mermaid is published as part of the Aistriú project which was funded by Galway 2020 as an element of the city's cultural programme as European Capital of Culture. The Aistriú project was led, coordinated, researched and supported on a voluntary basis by a team of scholars based in the National University of Ireland Galway. Most of the translators in this book were sourced via EFACIS, the European Federation of Associations and Centres of Irish Studies, while some were approached directly. The book is published by The Gallery Press, with the generous help and support of Literature Ireland.

Galway 2020: We wish to acknowledge the support of the Galway 2020 team over many years in contributing to the development, delivery and funding of the Aistriú project. In particular, we would like to thank Liz Kelly and Kate Howard, who acted as Cultural Producers at different stages of the project, as well as Galway 2020 Head of Programme, Marilyn Gaughan-Reddan.

NUI Galway: The Aistriú project was conceived in NUI Galway and it would not have succeeded without the generous voluntary support of the project team based in the University. It includes Dr Seán Crosson, Professor Louis de Paor, Susan Folan, Marianne Ní Chinnéide, Laoighseach Ní Choisdealbha, Dr Eilís Ní Dhúill, Séamus Ó Coileáin and Professor Lillis Ó Laoire. They freely shared their expertise in Irish literature, culture and translation, and we thank them most sincerely for their ideas, time and support. Thanks also to Trish Brennan for her administrative support early in the project.

EFACIS: We are indebted to the board of EFACIS and, in particular, to EFACIS Project Director, Hedwig Schwall, for their endorsement of this project. By reaching out through the EFACIS network the Aistriú project was able to attract a diverse mix of translators from across Europe and the world, and this book would not have been possible without the generous support of the EFACIS team.

The Gallery Press: Sincere thanks to Peter Fallon, founder and director of The Gallery Press, Suella Holland and their colleagues for their support. We couldn't ask for a better publisher and we thank them for their enthusiasm and expertise.

Literature Ireland: Sincere thanks to Literature Ireland Director, Sinéad Mac Aodha, for sharing her ideas and time so freely during the development of this book. Thanks to Literature Ireland also for their financial support which enabled us to appoint Peter Sirr as Translation Editor.

The Translators: We save our biggest 'thank you' for the Aistriú translators — a multilingual mix of scholars, poets and language enthusiasts from across the world who volunteered their time and creativity to translate the Aistriú texts from Irish and English into their own languages. Their generosity and enthusiasm sustained us throughout the Aistriú project, and this book is a tribute to a shared passion for language and literature.

Paul Muldoon's 'Translation Note' appeared in *Poetry* (*Translation Issue*) in 2007.

Dr John Caulfield and Professor Ríona Ní Fhrighil,
co-directors of the Aistriú project

Biographical Notes

Asma Saad Alshammari and Awatif Alshammari are native Arabic speakers and postgraduate students at the School of Languages, Literatures and Cultures, NUI Galway.

Li Yunru (李昀儒) is a native speaker of Chinese and an MA student at the Irish Studies Centre, School of English and International Studies, Beijing Foreign Studies University.

Martin Světlík is a translator and literary editor based in Prague, Czechia.

Benjamin Van Pottelbergh is a graduate in translation and multilingual business communication and is currently working as a content creator in Ghent, Belgium.

Audrey Robitaillié is a literary and folklore scholar based around the Irish and Celtic seas, washing up on Scottish, Irish or French shores depending on the seasons. Daniel McAuley is an English and French scholar based at Aston University in Birmingham, England.

Jorge Rodríguez Durán is an Irish Studies scholar, translator and poet based in Santiago de Compostela, Spain.

Arndt Wigger is a linguist and Celtic scholar based in Königswinter, Germany.

Natasha Remoundou is an academic researcher, literary scholar, lecturer and writer based in Ireland.

Mitsuko Ohno is Aichi Shukutoku University's Professor Emerita and, as a translator, has published poetry books in Japan and Ireland.

Jerzy Jarniewicz is a poet and literary scholar based in Łódź, Poland.

Magdalena Kleszczewska is a literary translator, literarian and Irish enthusiast based in Warsaw, Poland. She holds a degree in Anglo-Irish Literature and Culture. Warsaw born, Radom raised, she has Droim Conrach written in her heart.

Barbara Szot is a Gaeilgeoir in progress based in Olomouc, Czech Republic.

Hugo Sousa is a master's student of Translation and Multilingual Communication at the University of Minho. He has a

Bachelor of Arts degree in Languages and Literatures and is fluent in English and Spanish in addition to his mother tongue, Portuguese.

Carolina Carvalho holds a degree in Applied Languages and is a master's student of Translation and Multilingual Communication at the University of Minho. She has proficiency in English, Spanish, and German, as well as Portuguese.

Luís Ramos is a freelance translator and musician from Santo Tirso, Portugal. He is currently taking a master's degree in Translation and Multilingual Communication at the University of Minho after finishing his Bachelor of Arts degree in Languages, Literatures and Cultures at the University of Porto. He is fluent in Portuguese, English and German.

Maria Filomena Louro is Associate Professor at University of Minho. She created the MA degree in Translation and Multilingual Communication. Her research interests are Irish Literature and Theatre. She is a co-founder of EFACIS.